15 14 13 12 11 10 09 08   8 7 6 5 4 3 2 1

Adult Coloring Book
A Stress Relieving Inspirational Adventure
Original designs by Reverend Bonnie McPhail
Copyright © 2018

Bonnie McPhail

Creatspace Publishers

Dear Friends,

This beautifully illustrated coloring book is my first attempt at using my own sketches and is designed for hours of relaxing enjoyment with some of the pages containing inspirational favorite scripture verses. These are all original drawings and my hope is that they will be a fun adventure as you work on them. You will find some of them very detailed and will provide hours worth of enjoyment and others that are simple and take only a few minutes. There is something for everyone!

Blessings to all!
From my heart to yours...
Pastor Bonnie

Adult Coloring Book

A Stress Relieving Inspirational Adventure

By

Reverend Bonnie McPhail

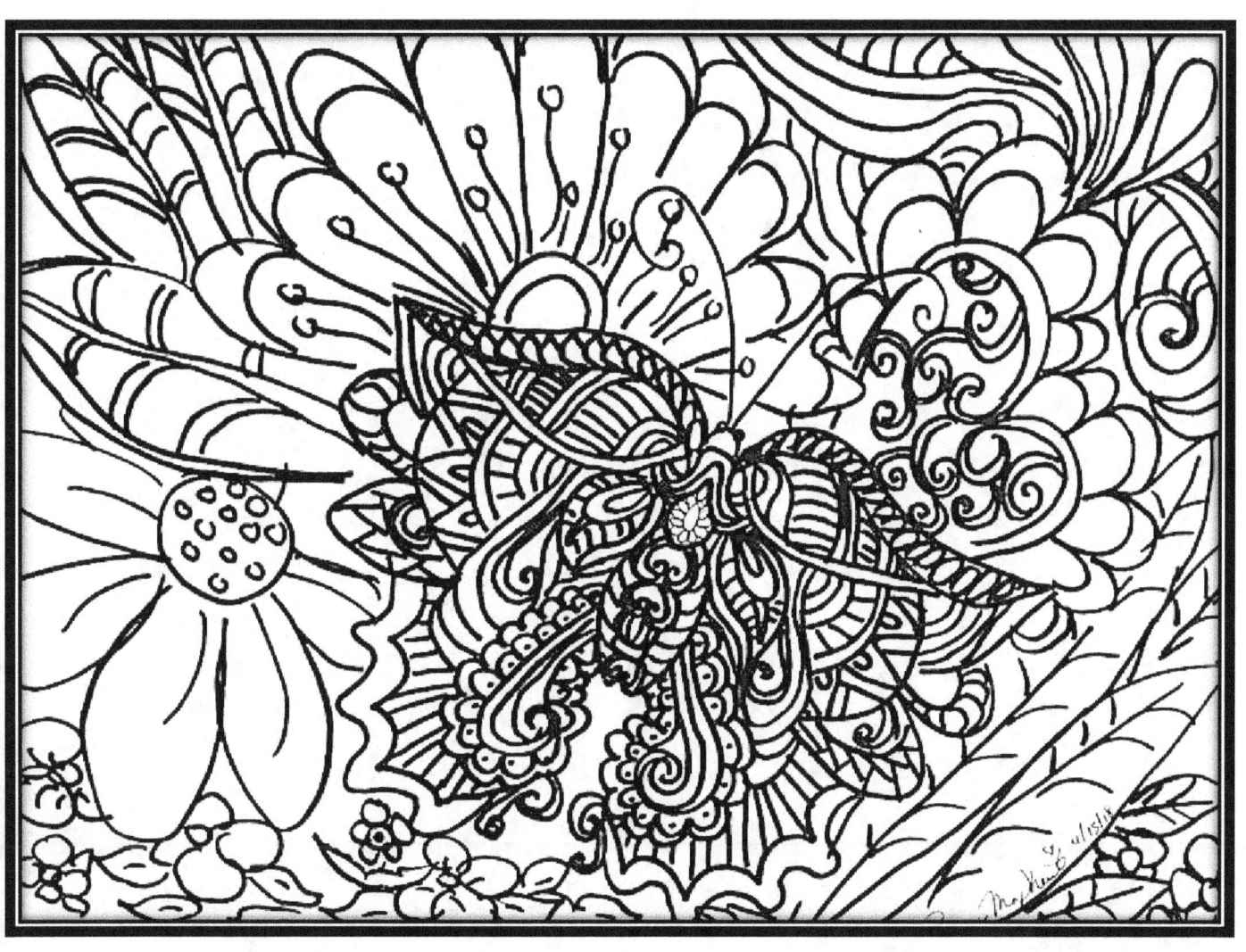

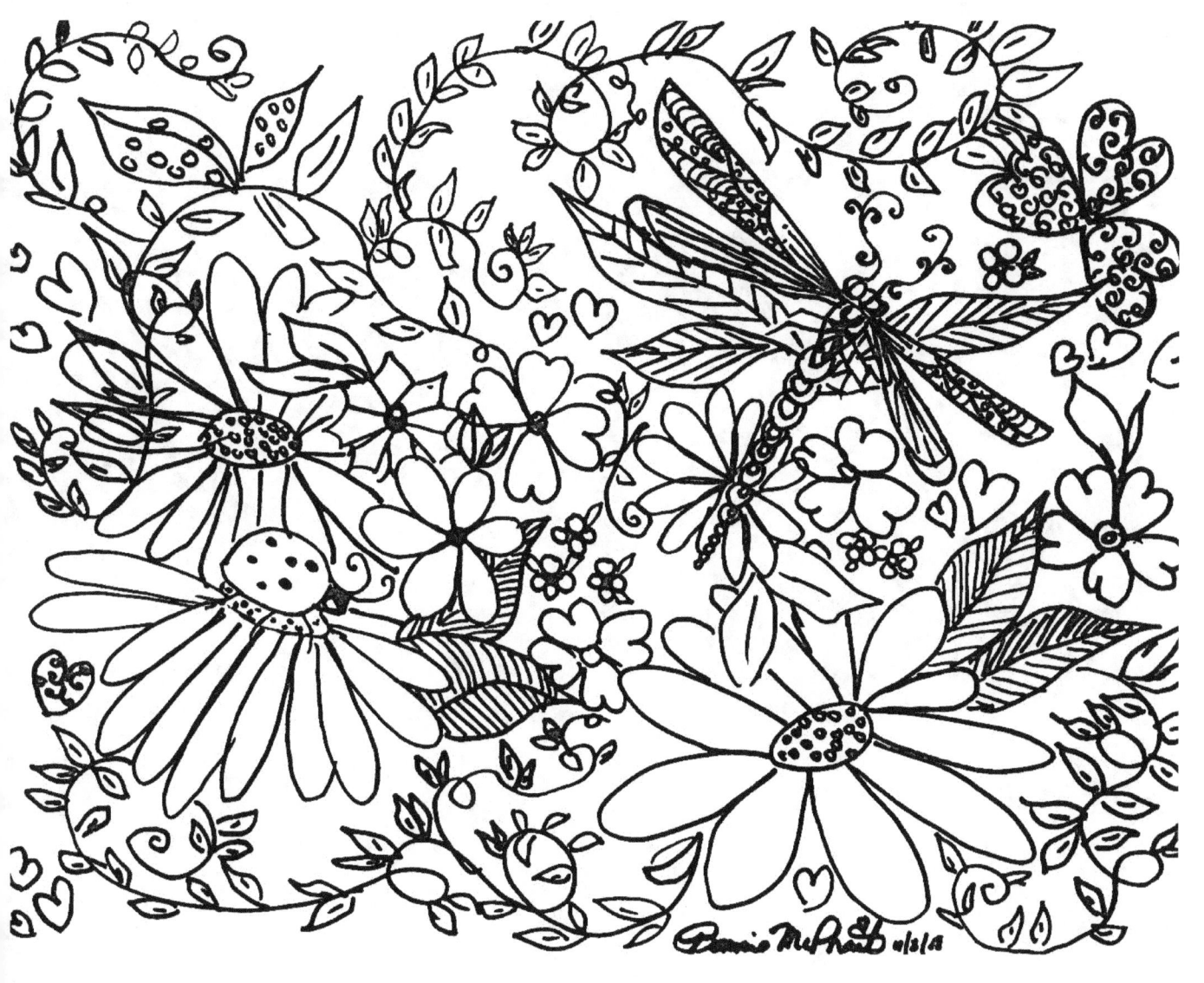

The Lord is my shepherd, I lack nothing.

Psalm 23:1

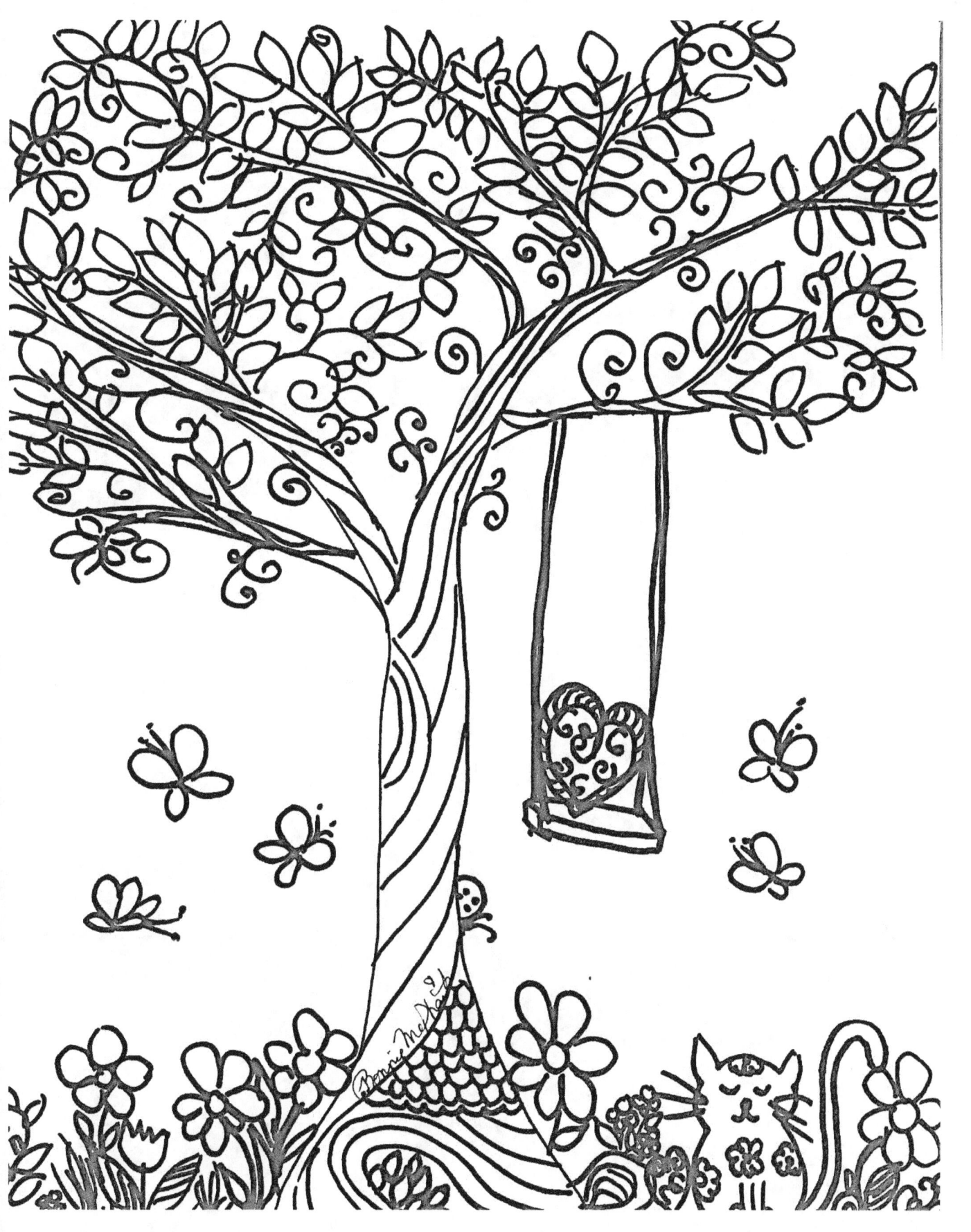

"He makes me lie down in green pastures,

he leads me beside quiet waters,

he refreshes my soul."

Psalm 23:2

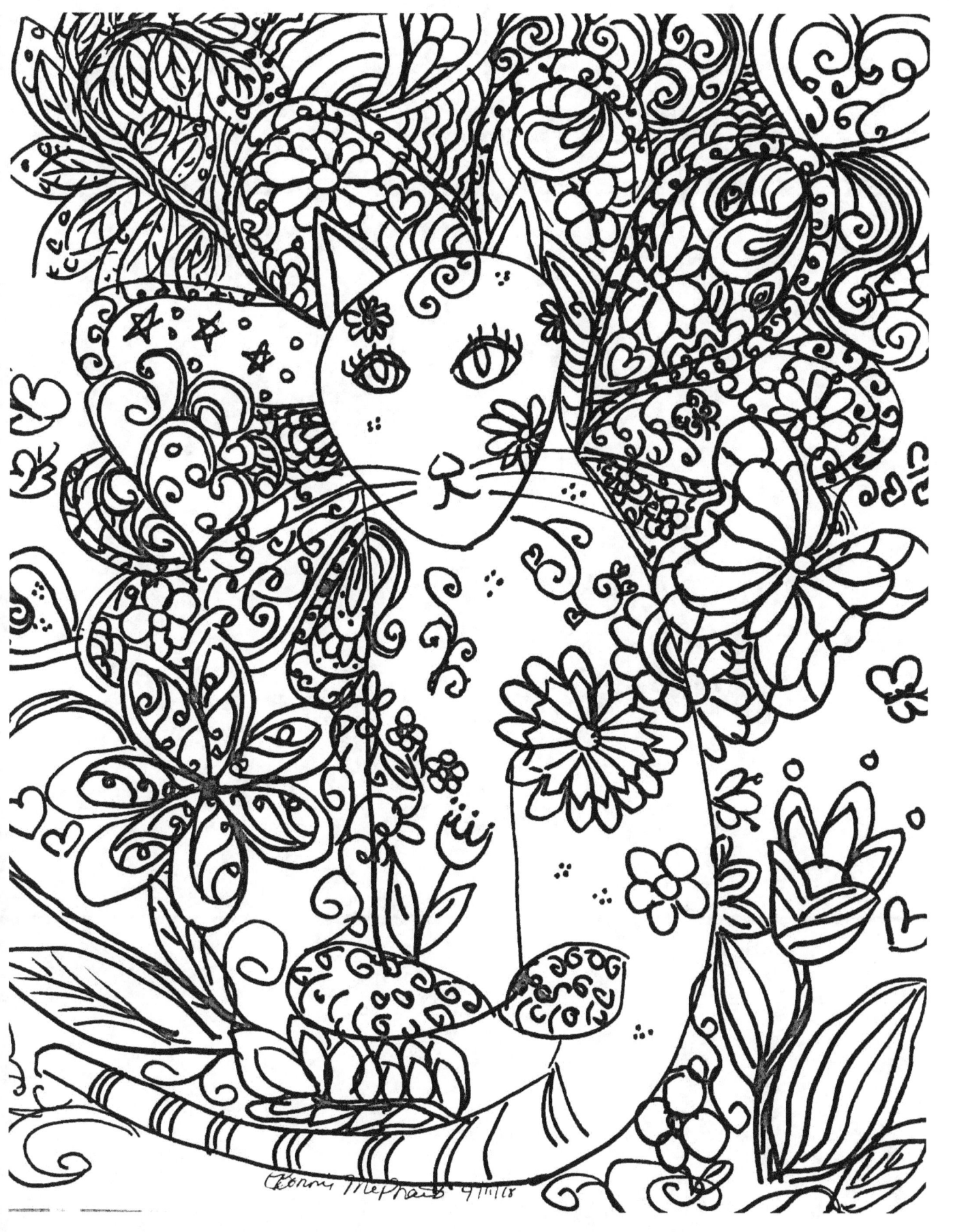

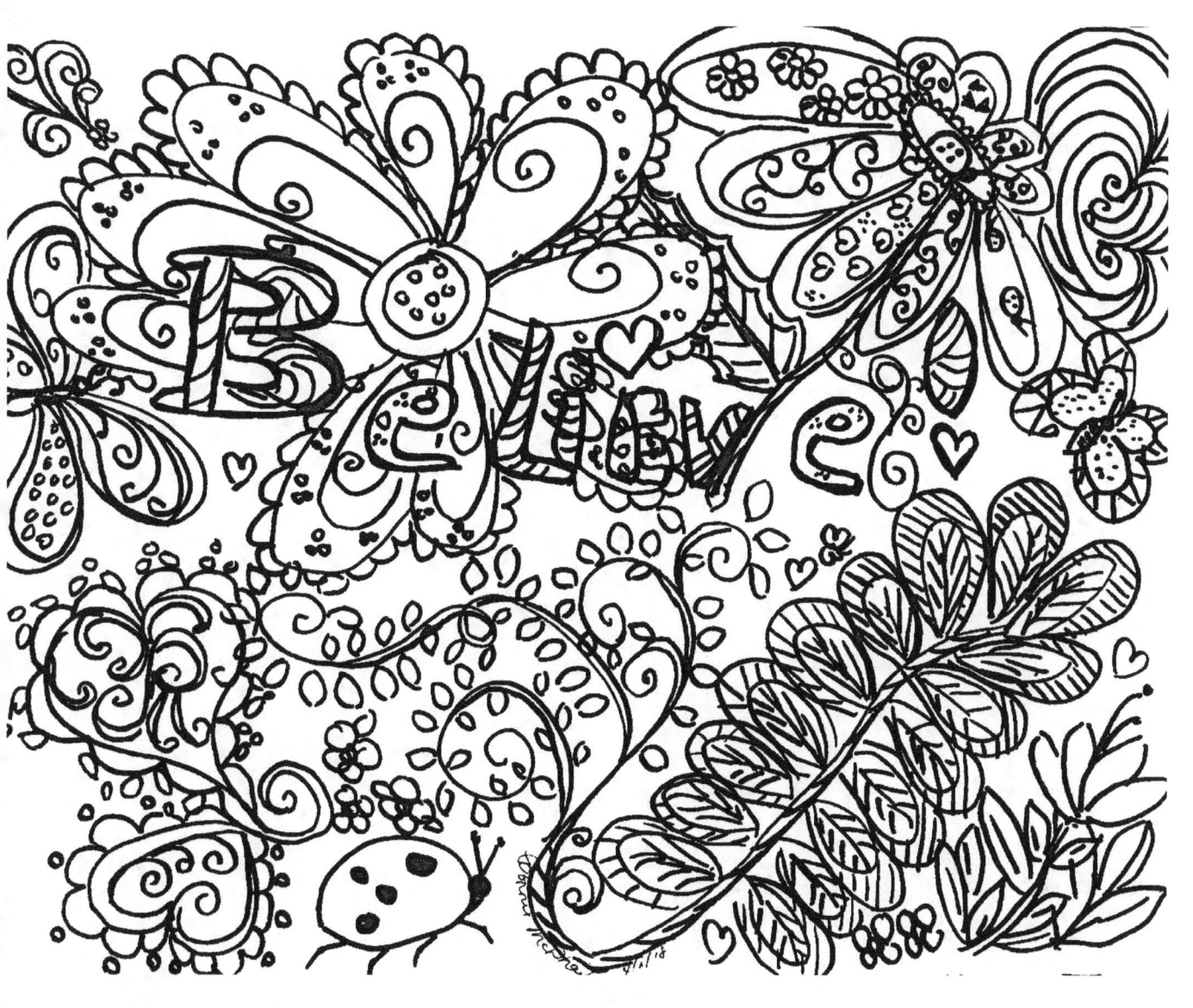

"He refreshes my soul.

He guides me along the right paths for his name's sake."

Psalm 23:3

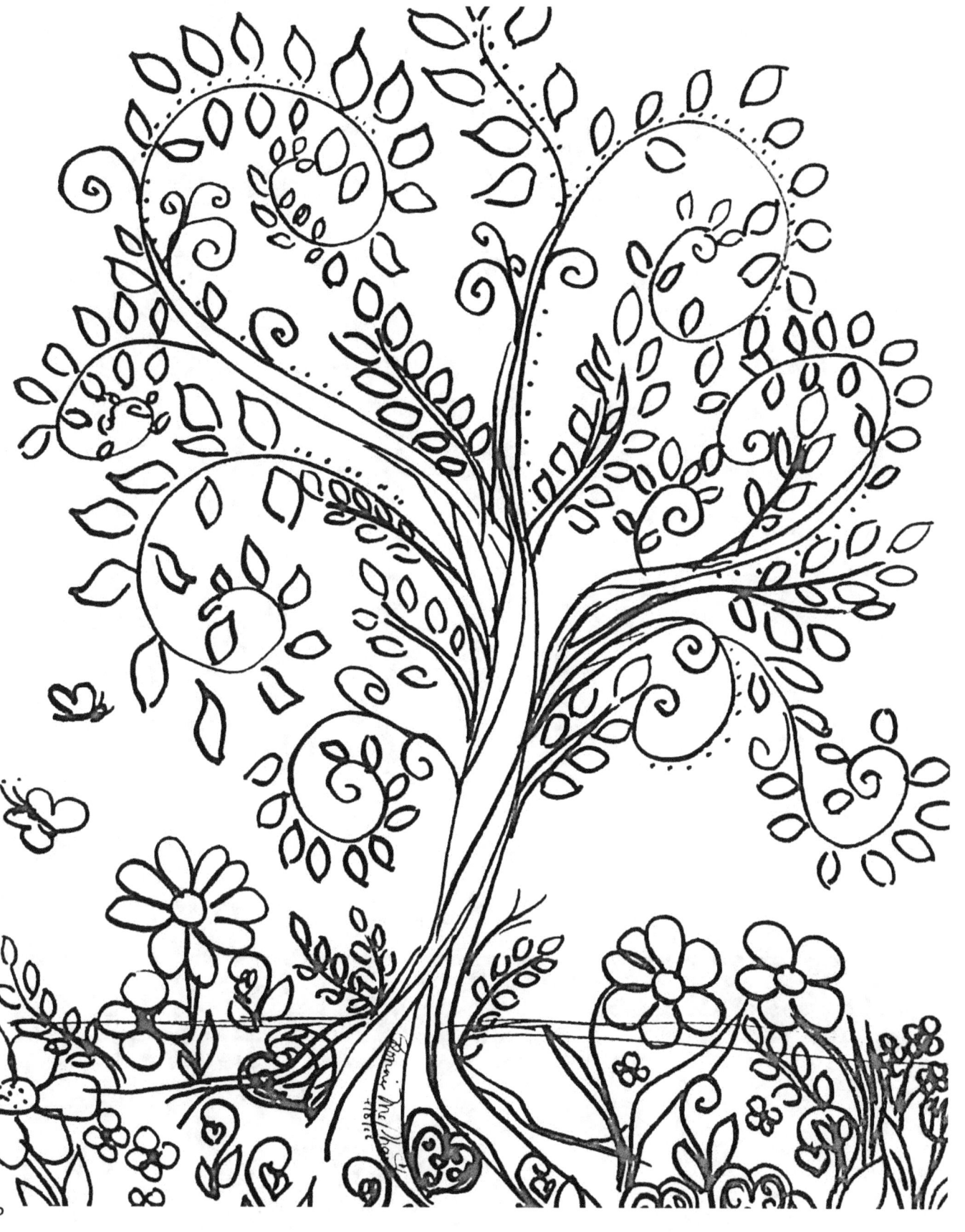

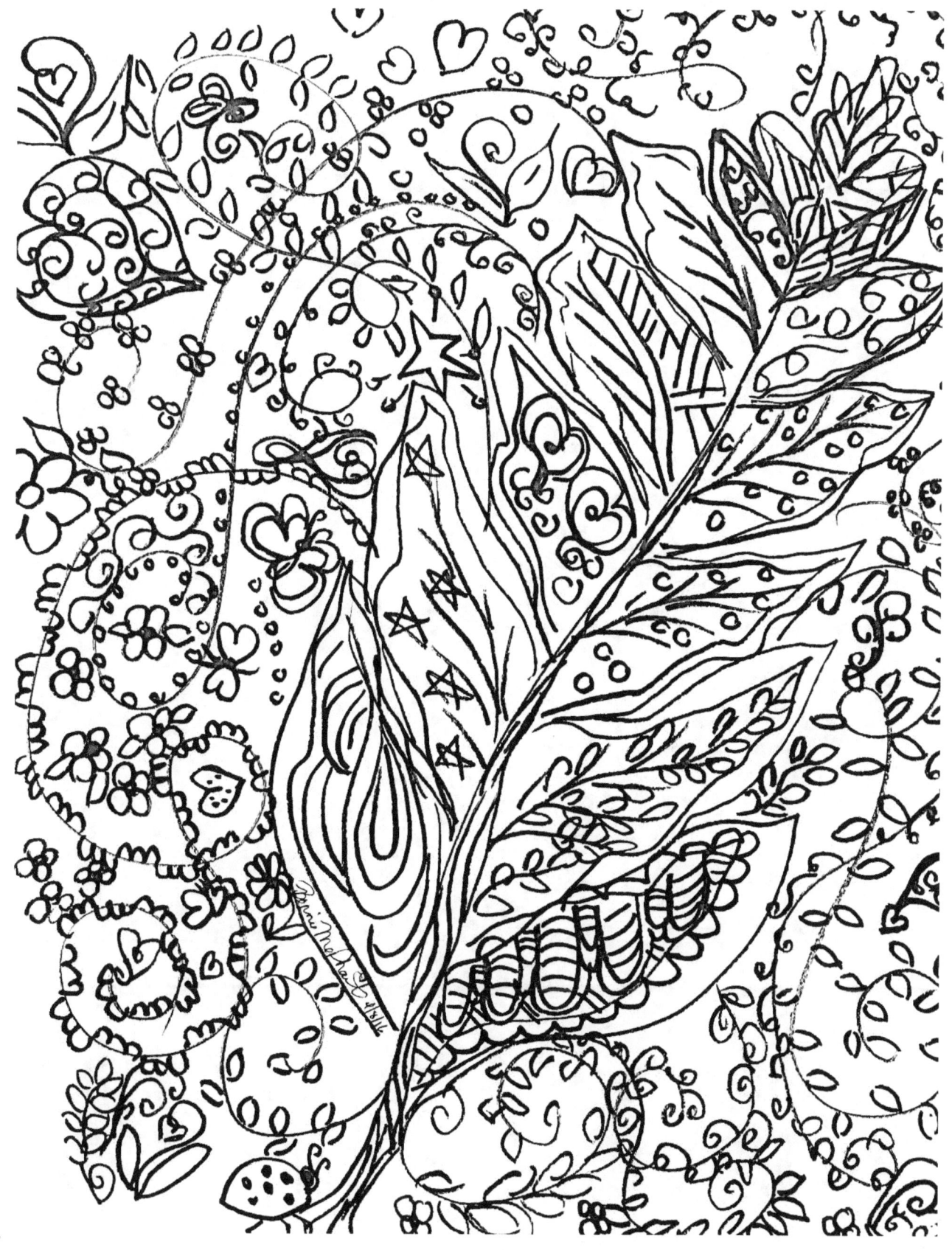

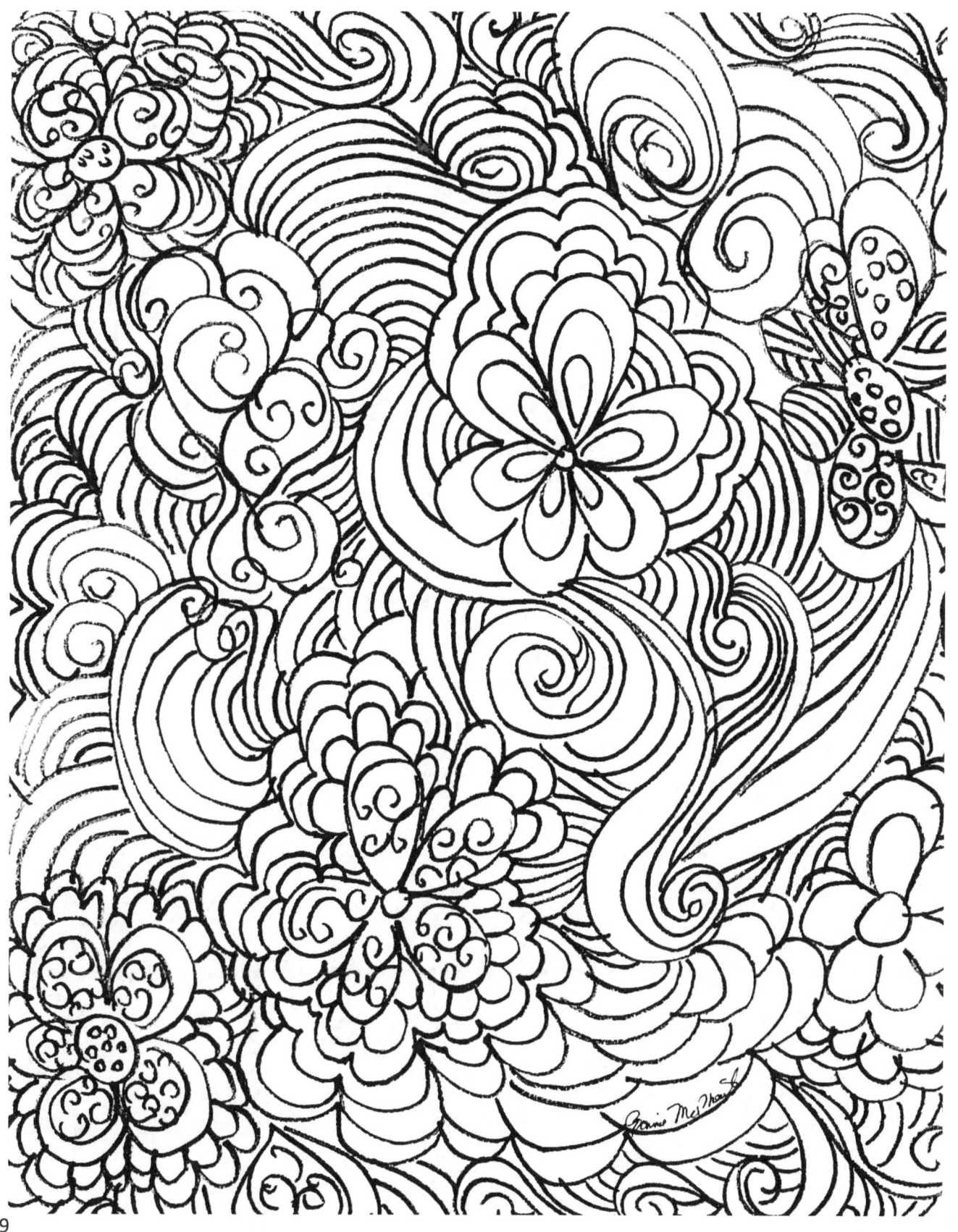

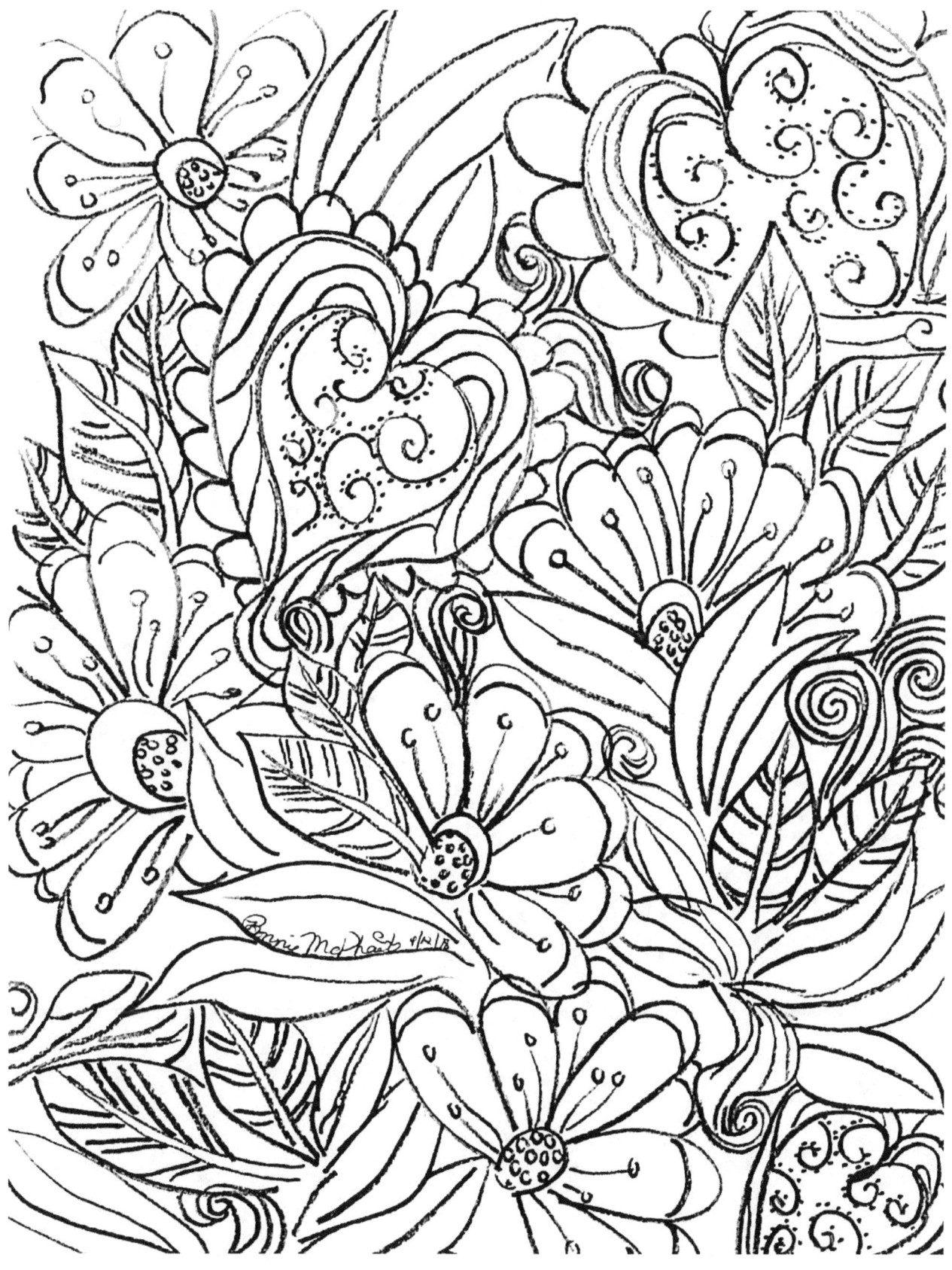

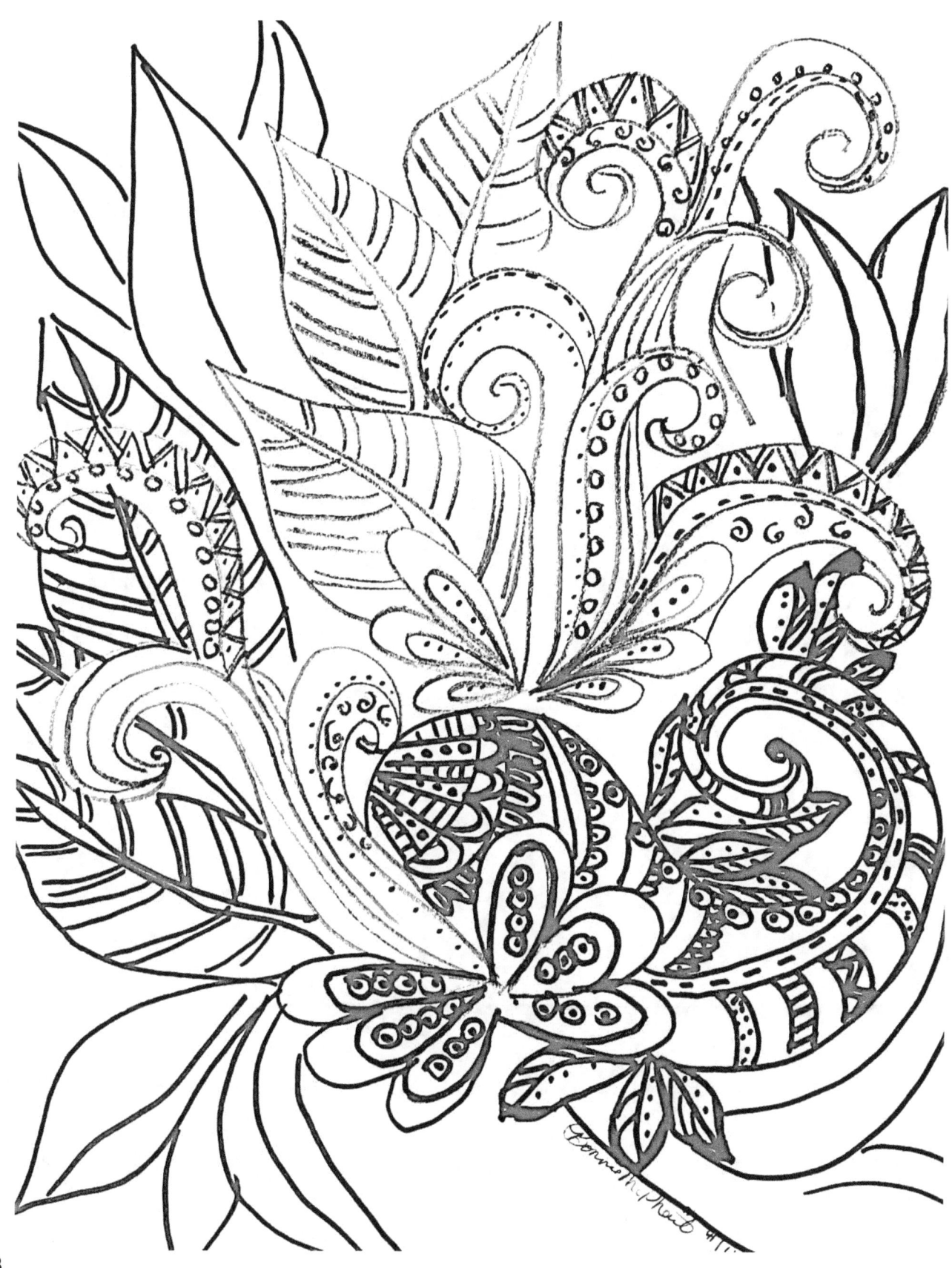

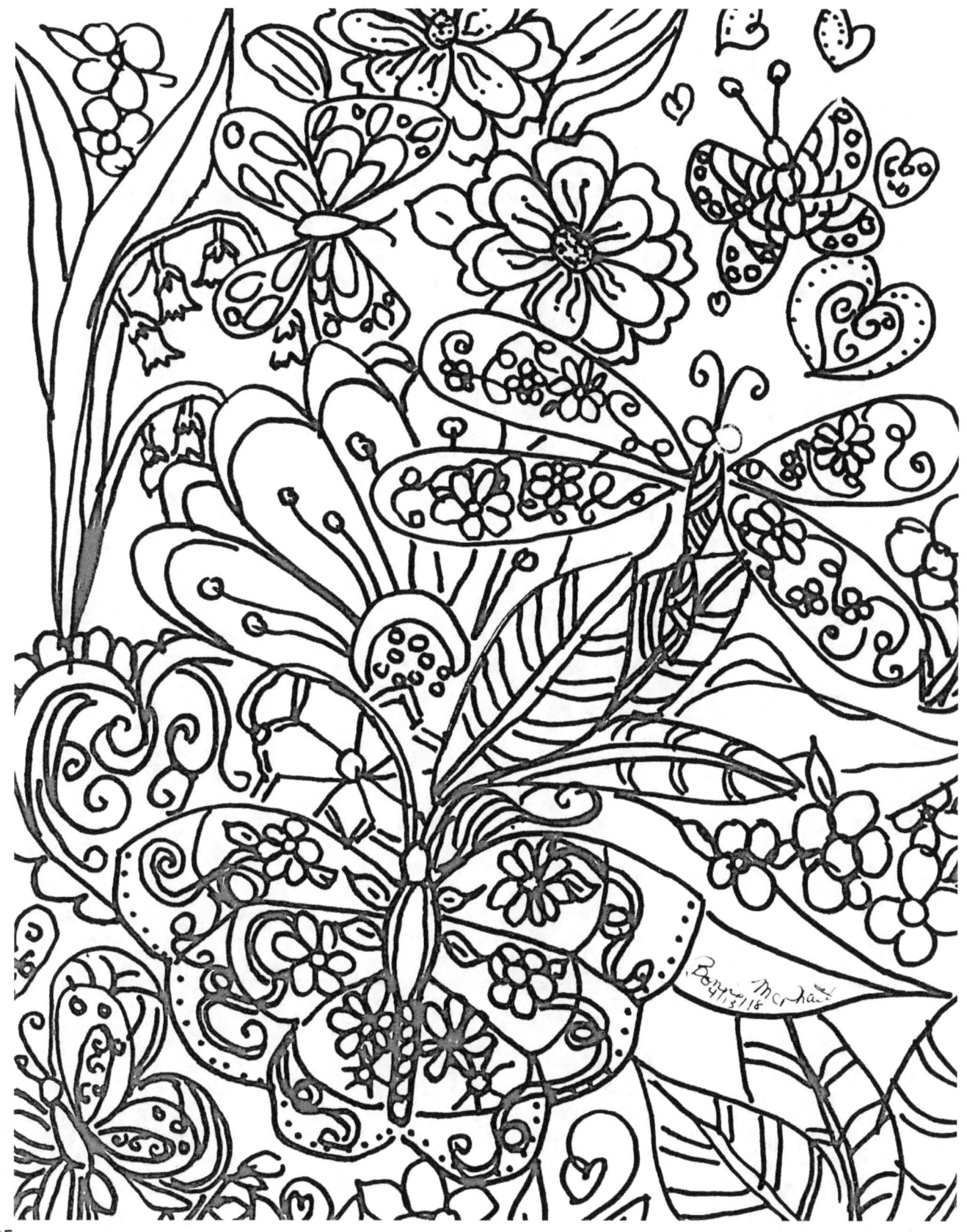

"Even though I walk through the darkest valley,

I will fear no evil, for you are with me;

Your rod and your staff,

They comfort me."

Psalm 23:4

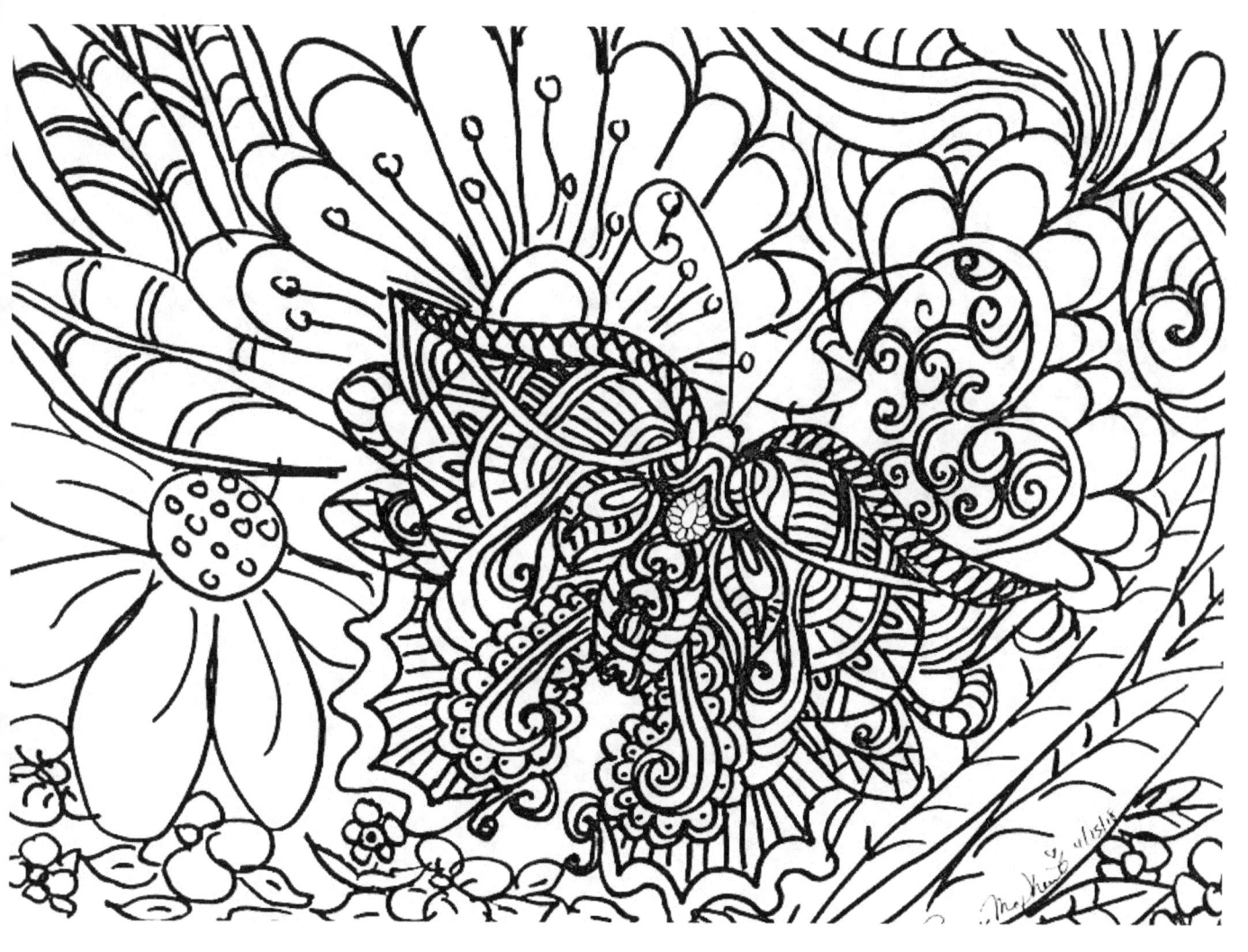

"You prepare a table before me in the presence of my enemies.

You anoint my head with oil; my cup overflows."

Psalm 23:5

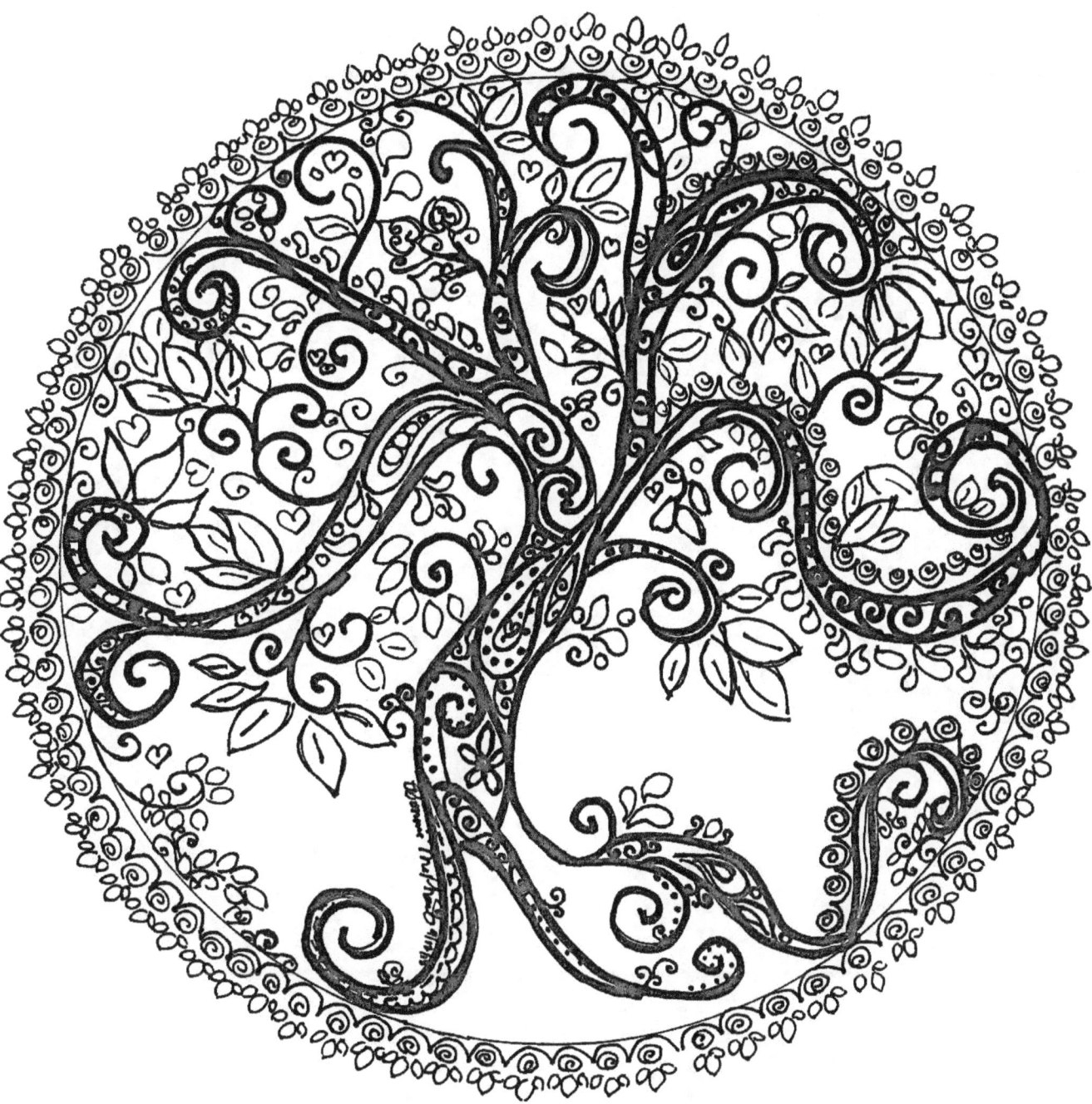

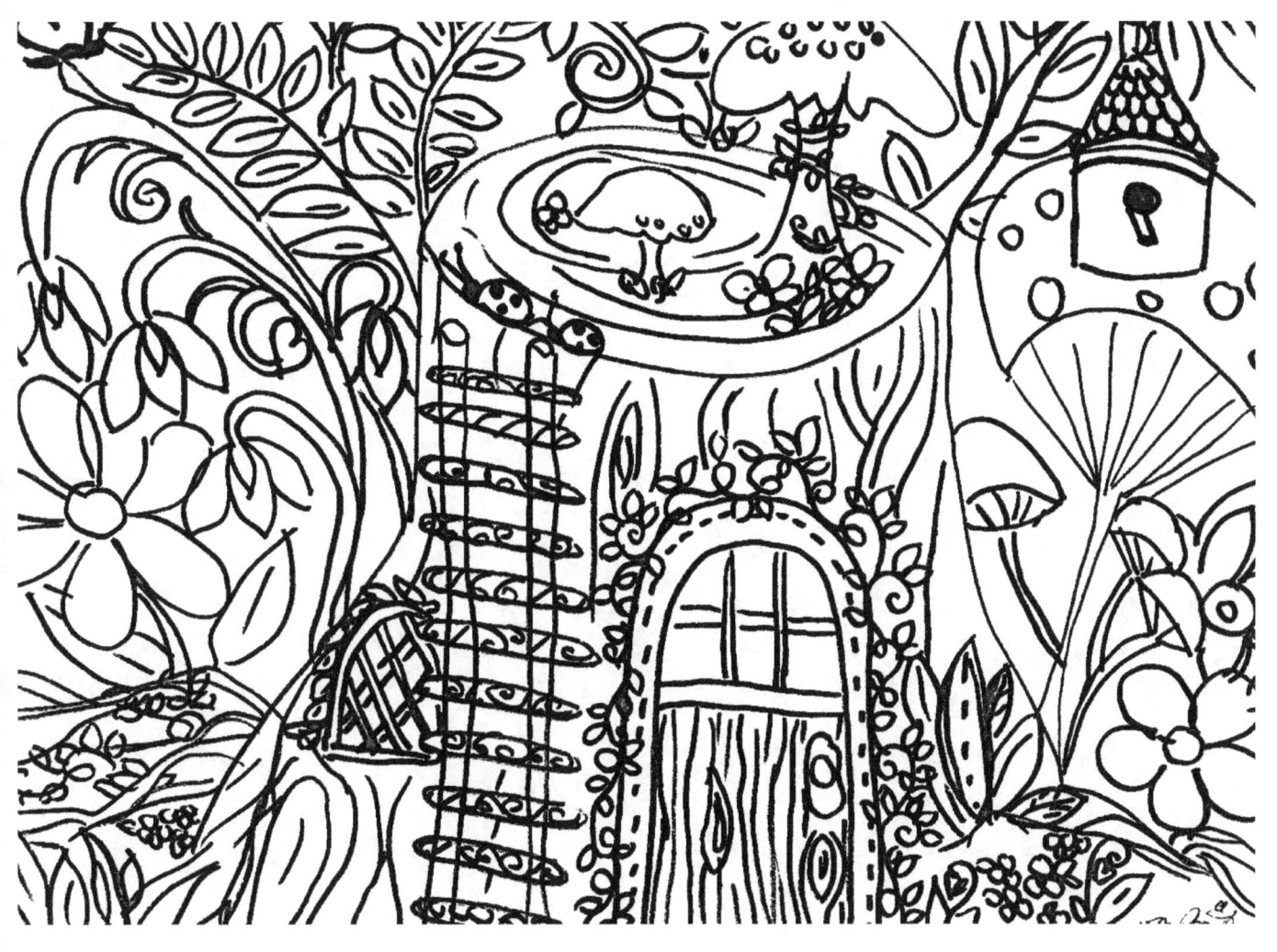

"Surely your goodness and love will follow me all the days of my life,

And I will dwell in the house of the Lord forever."

Psalm 23:6

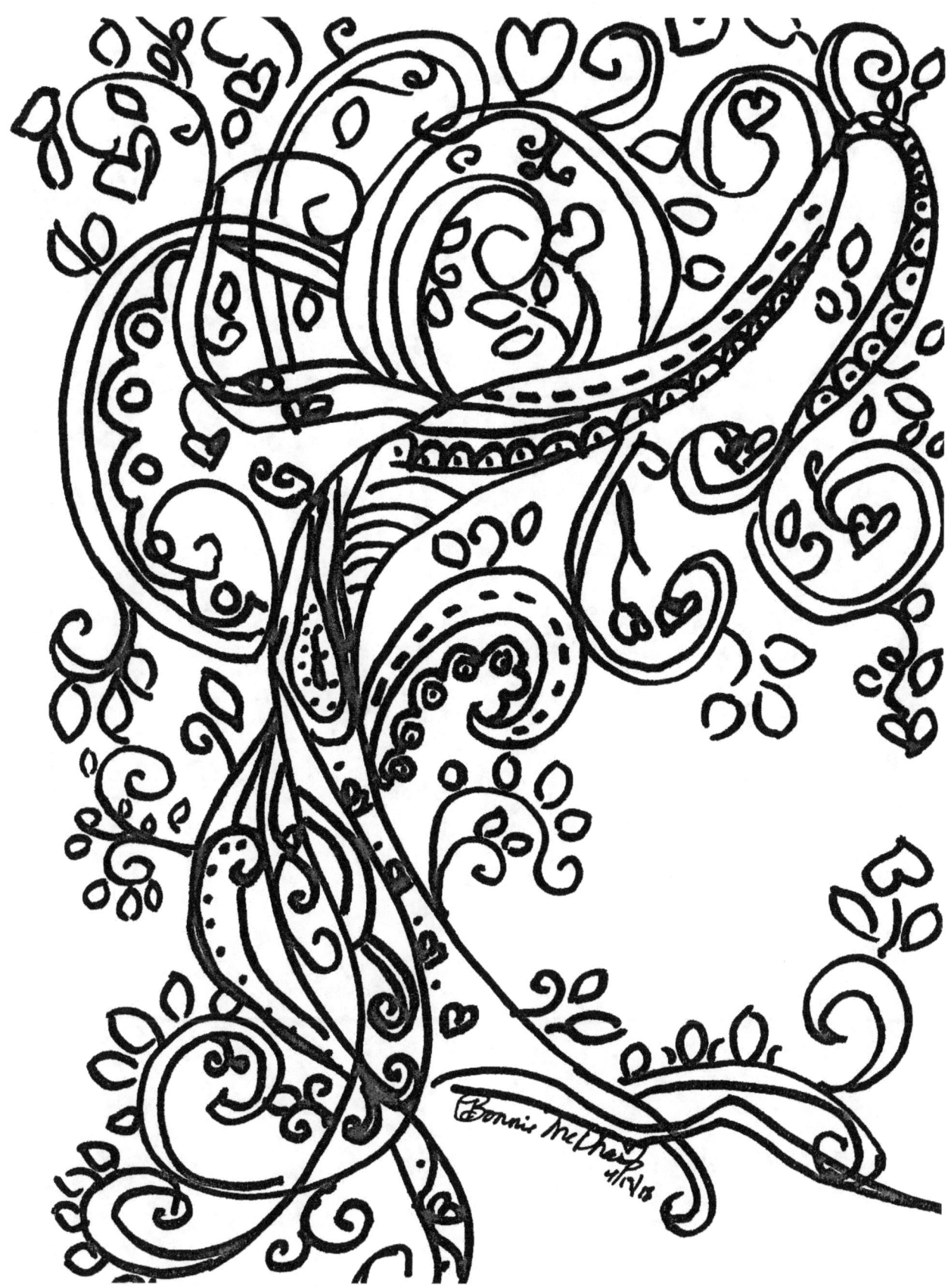

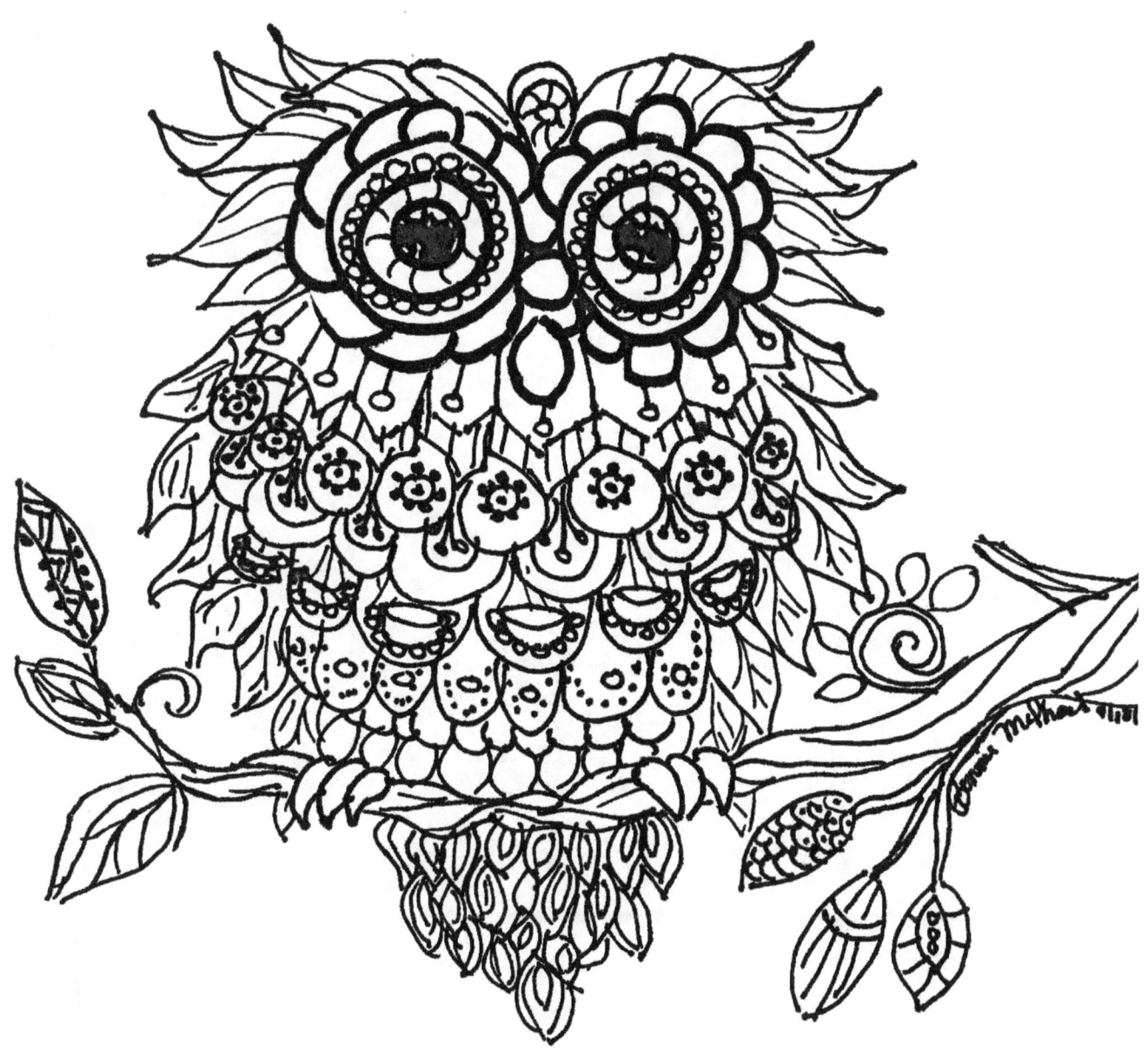

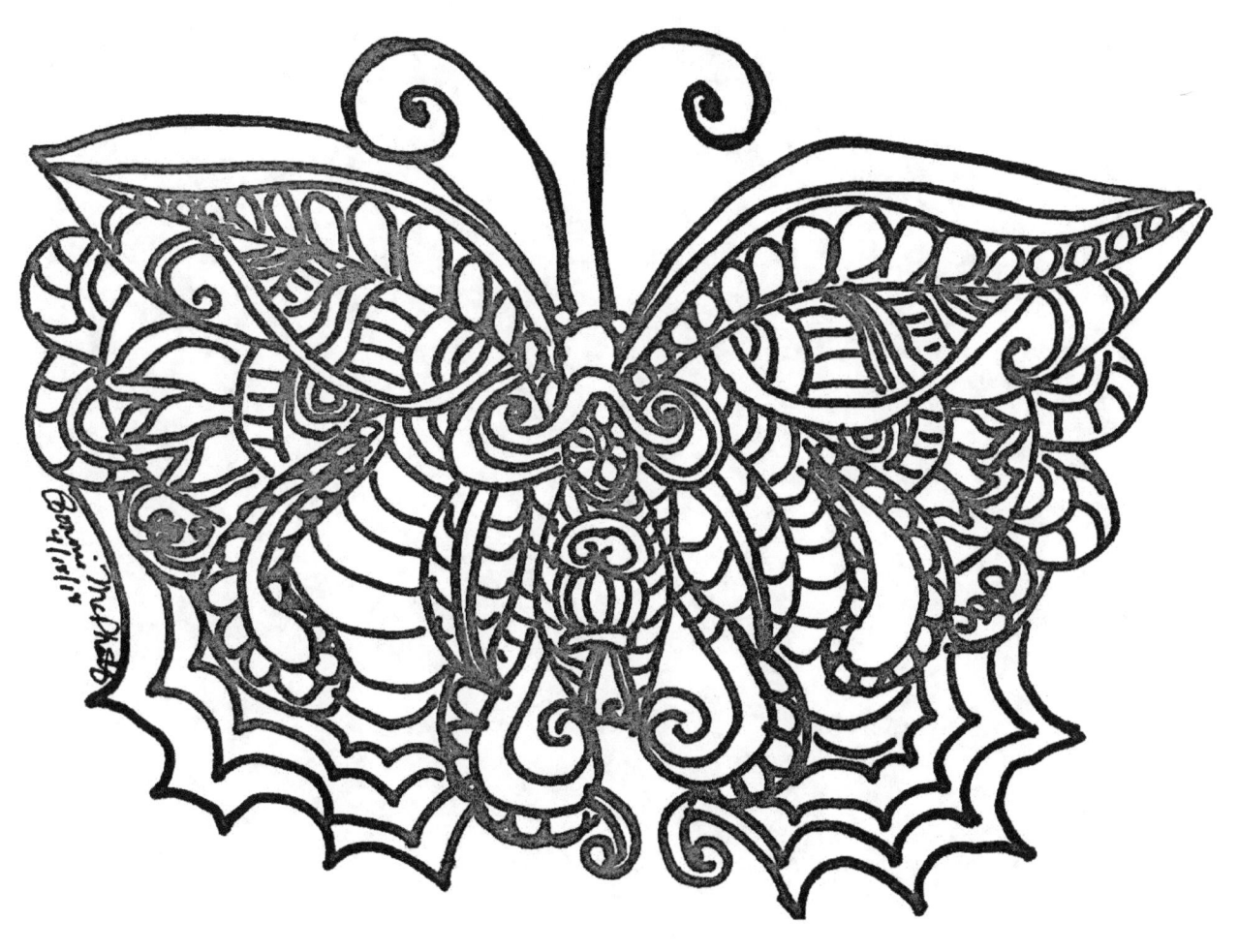

"O LORD, you have searched me and known me!

You know when I sit down and when I rise up;

you discern my thoughts from afar."

Psalm 139: 1-2

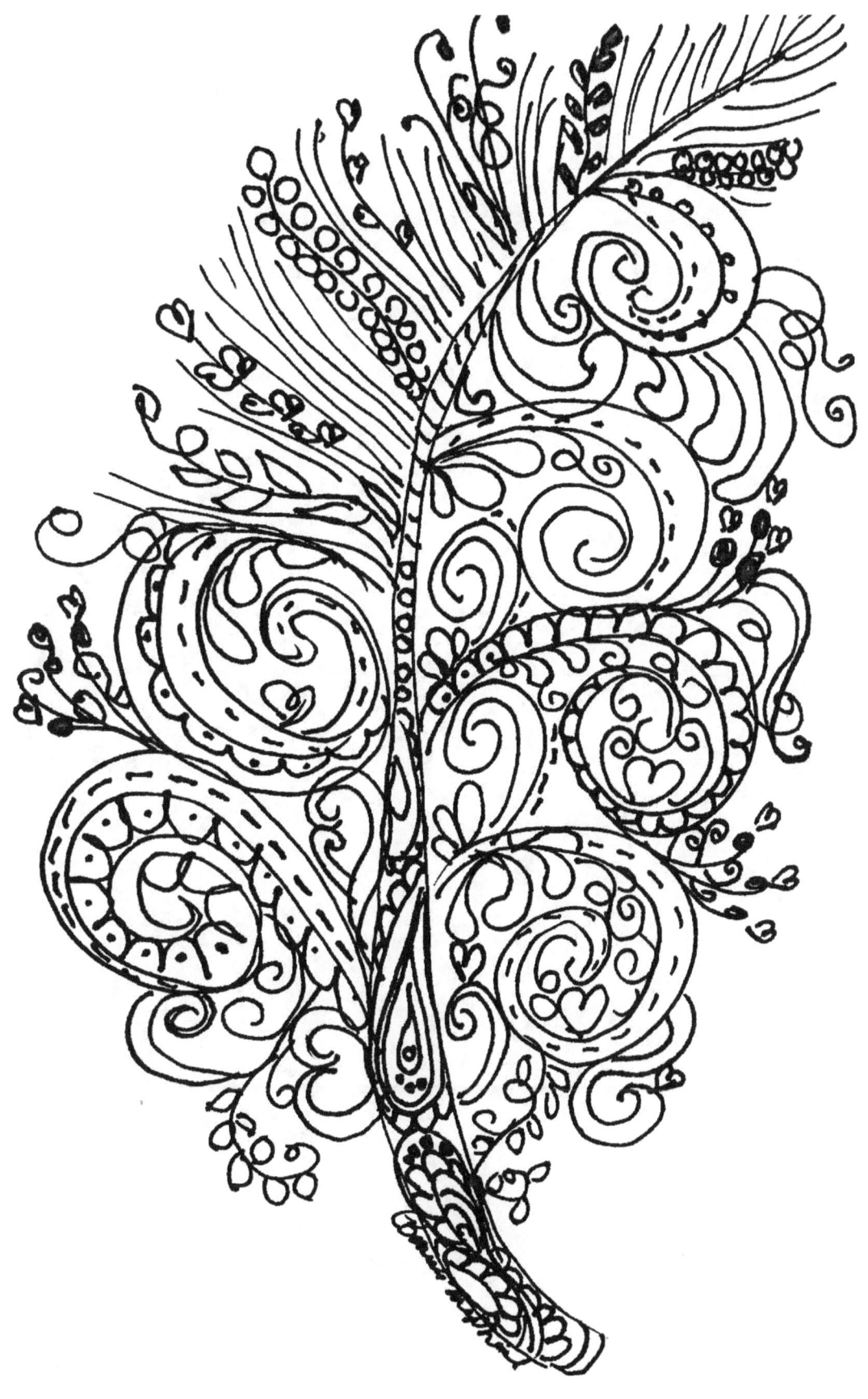

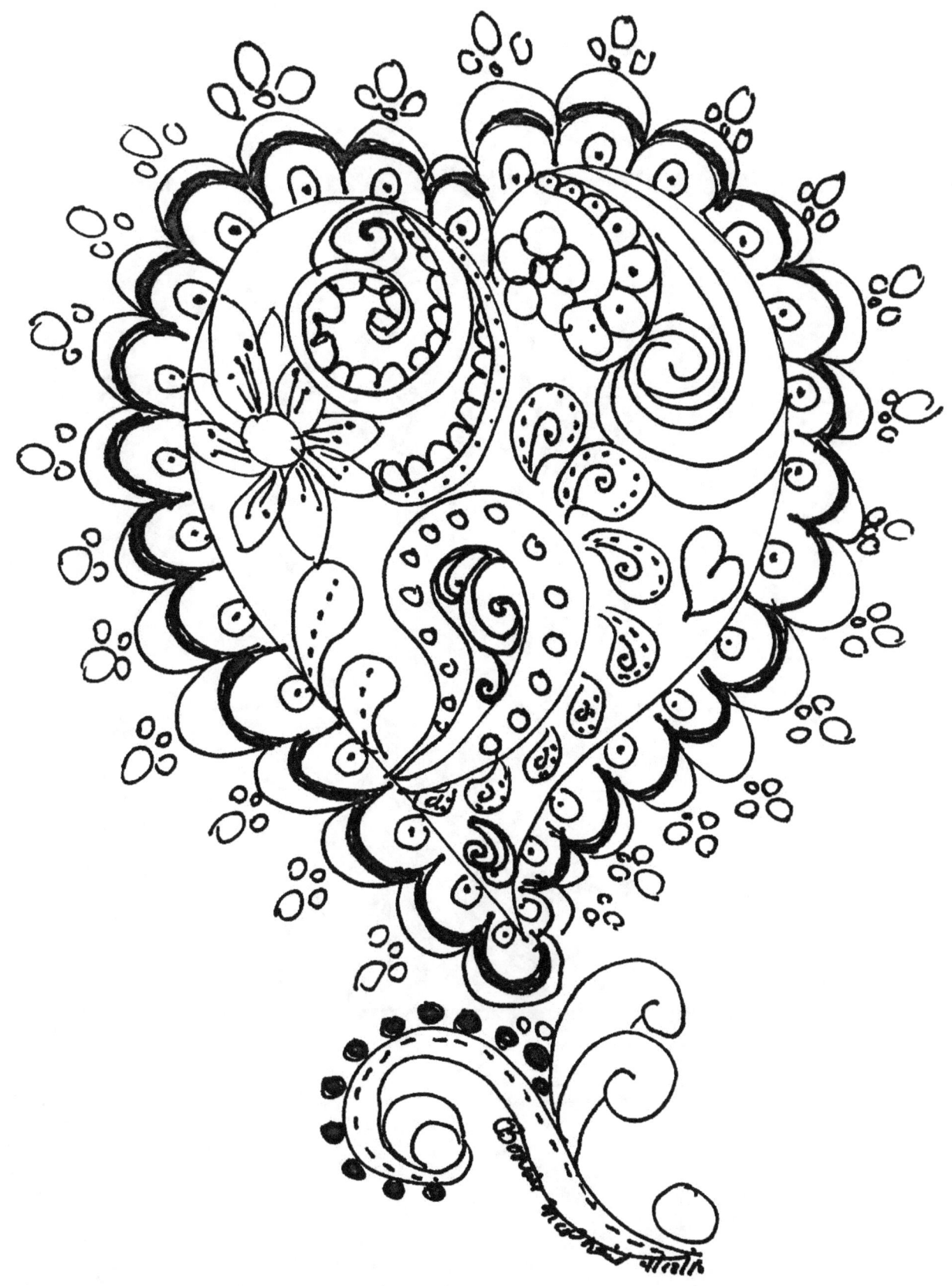

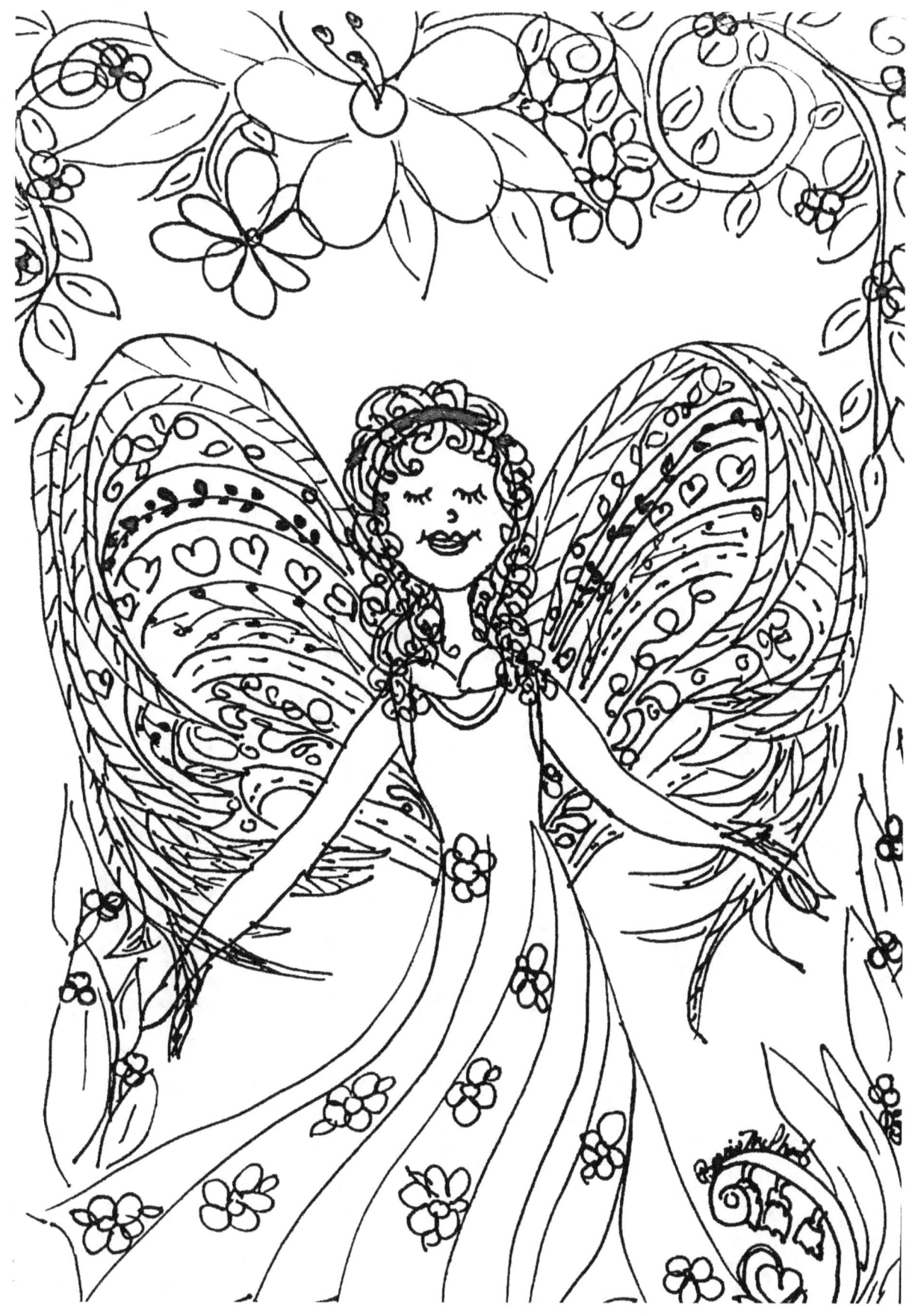

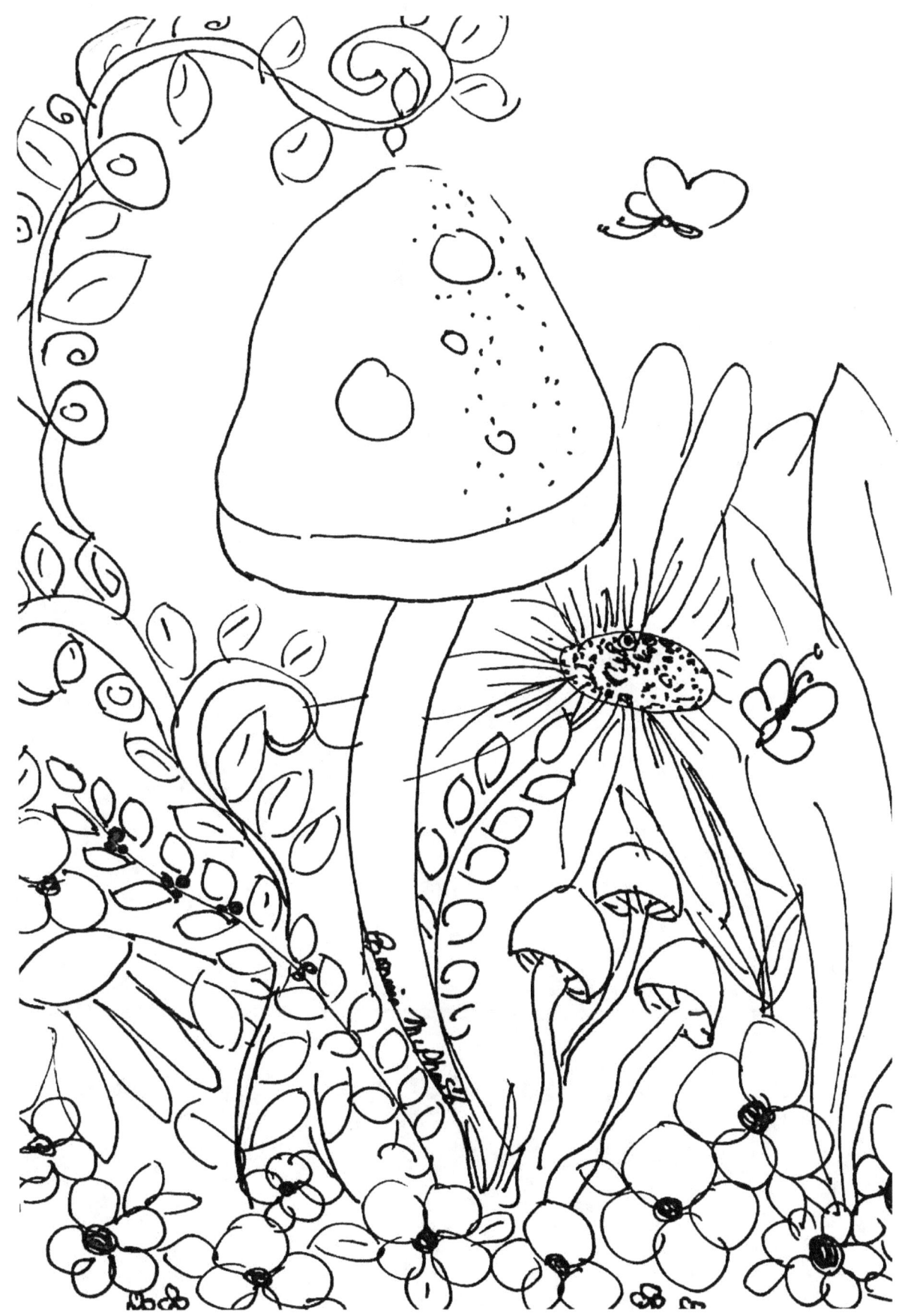

51

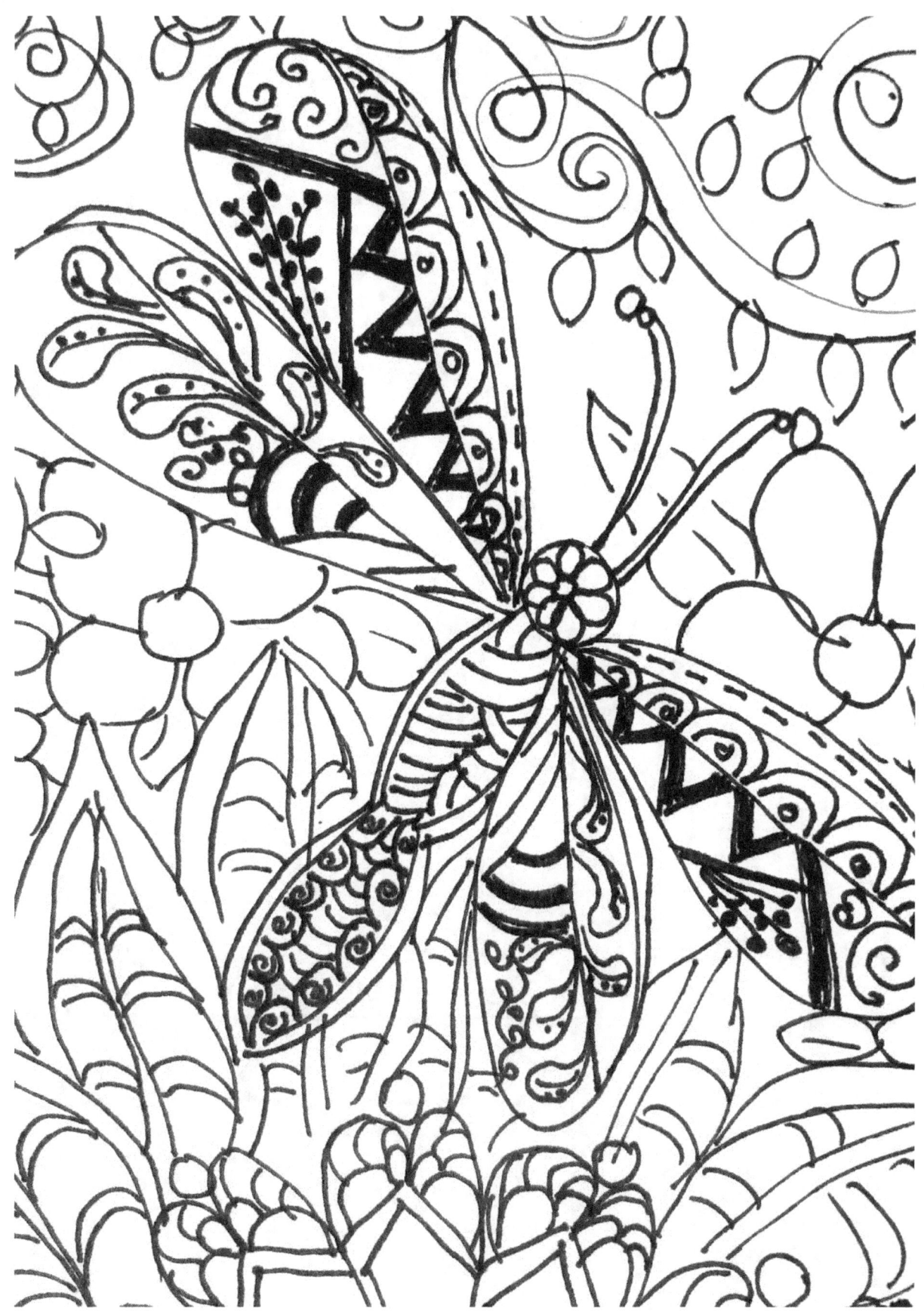

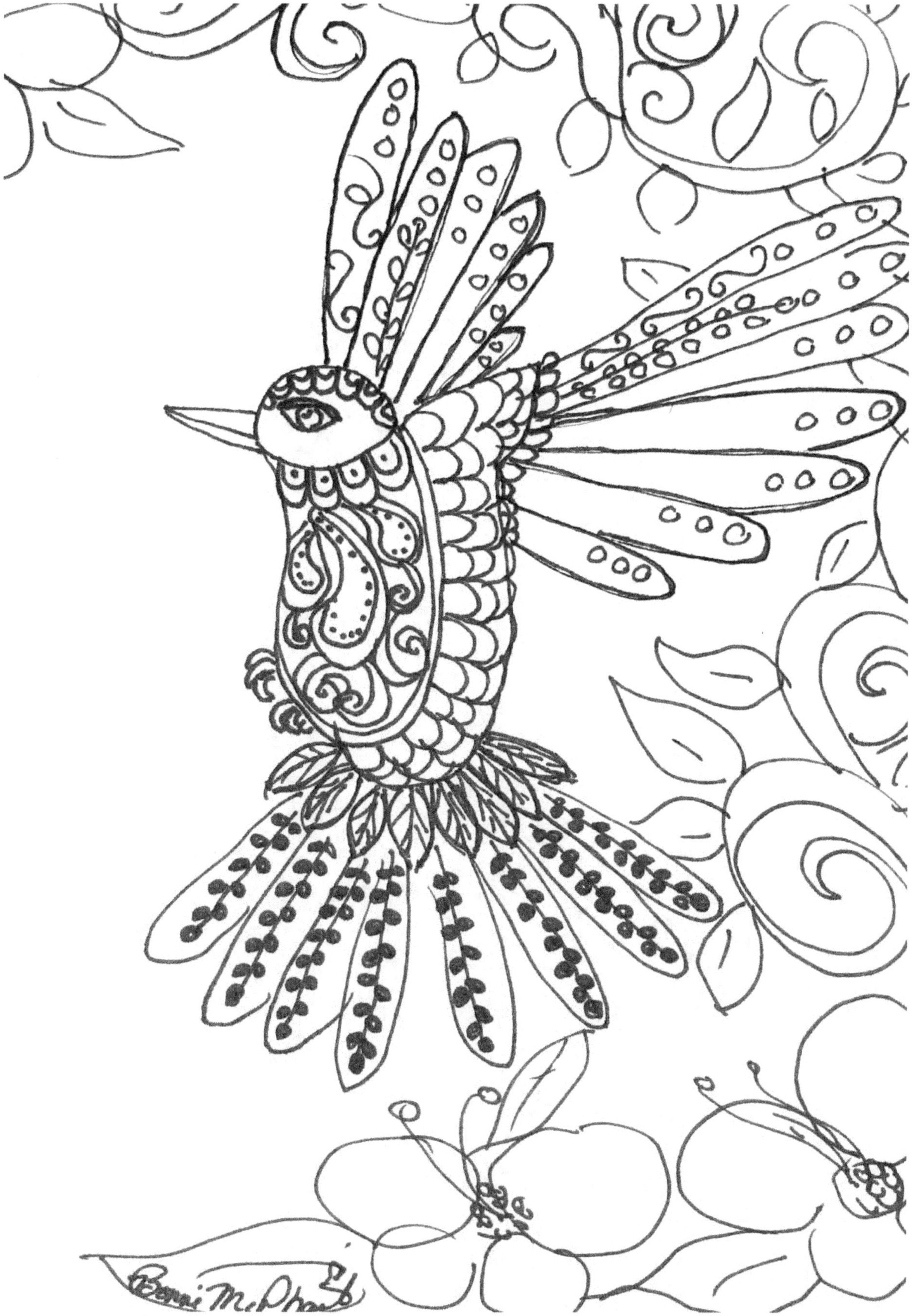

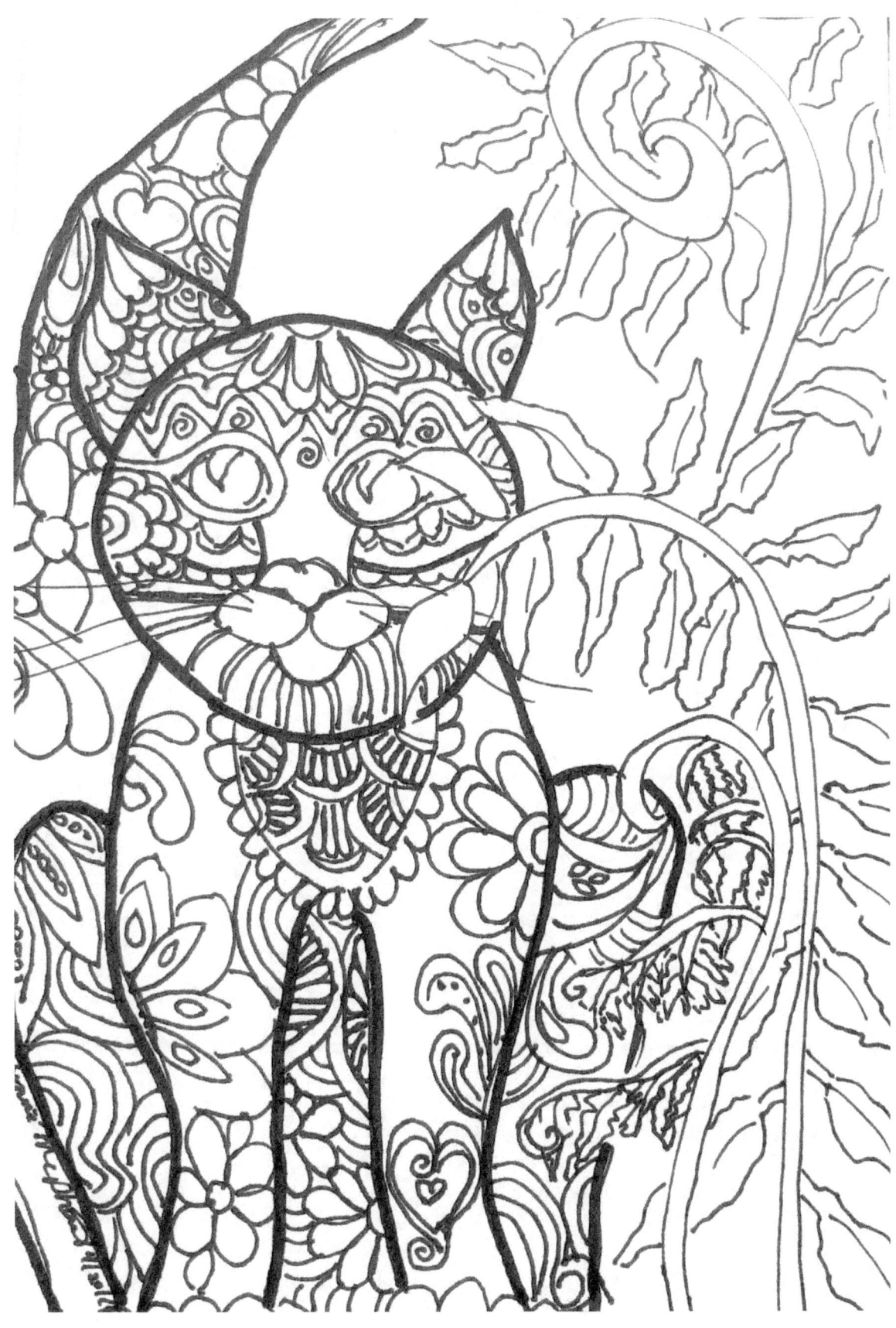

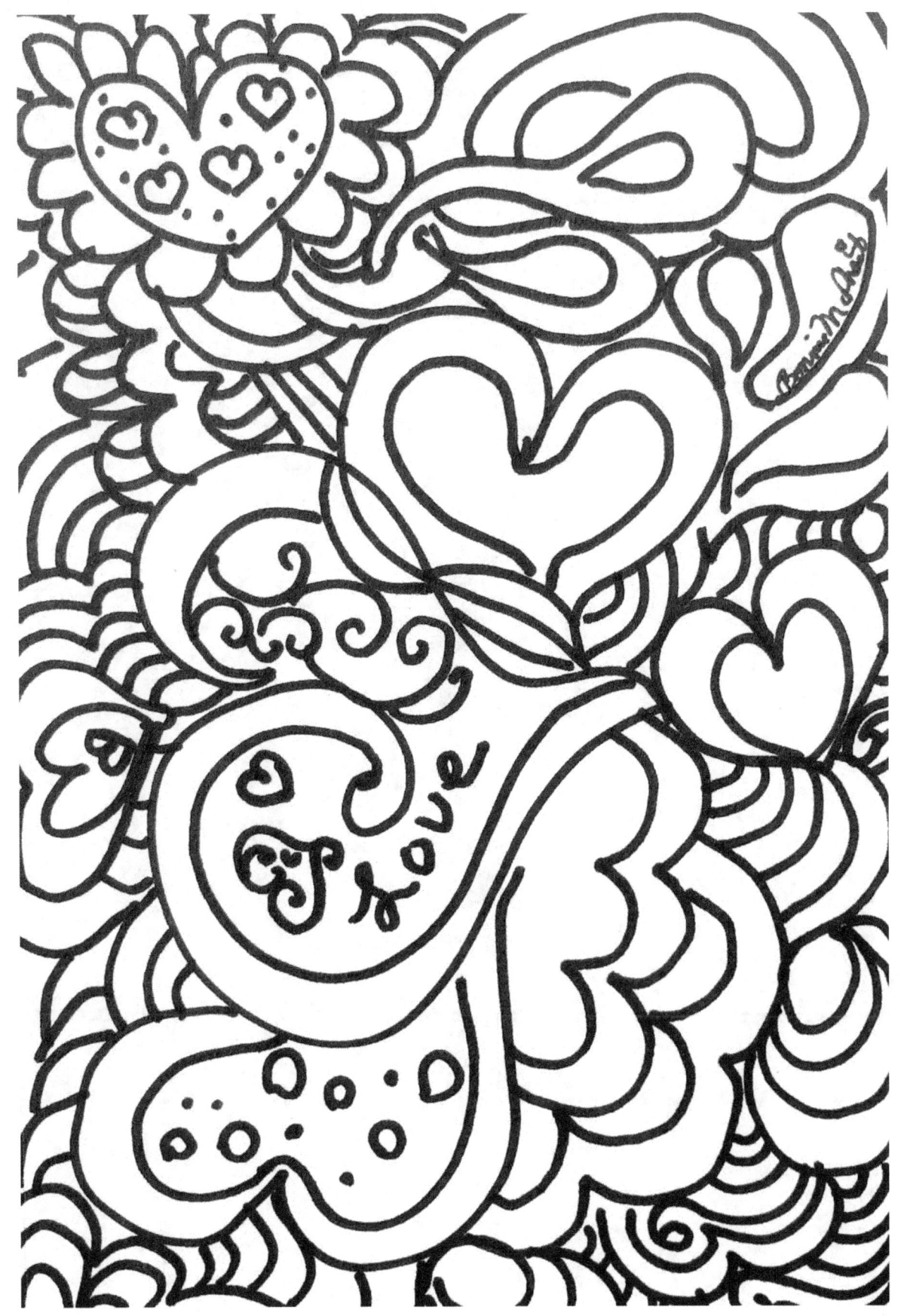

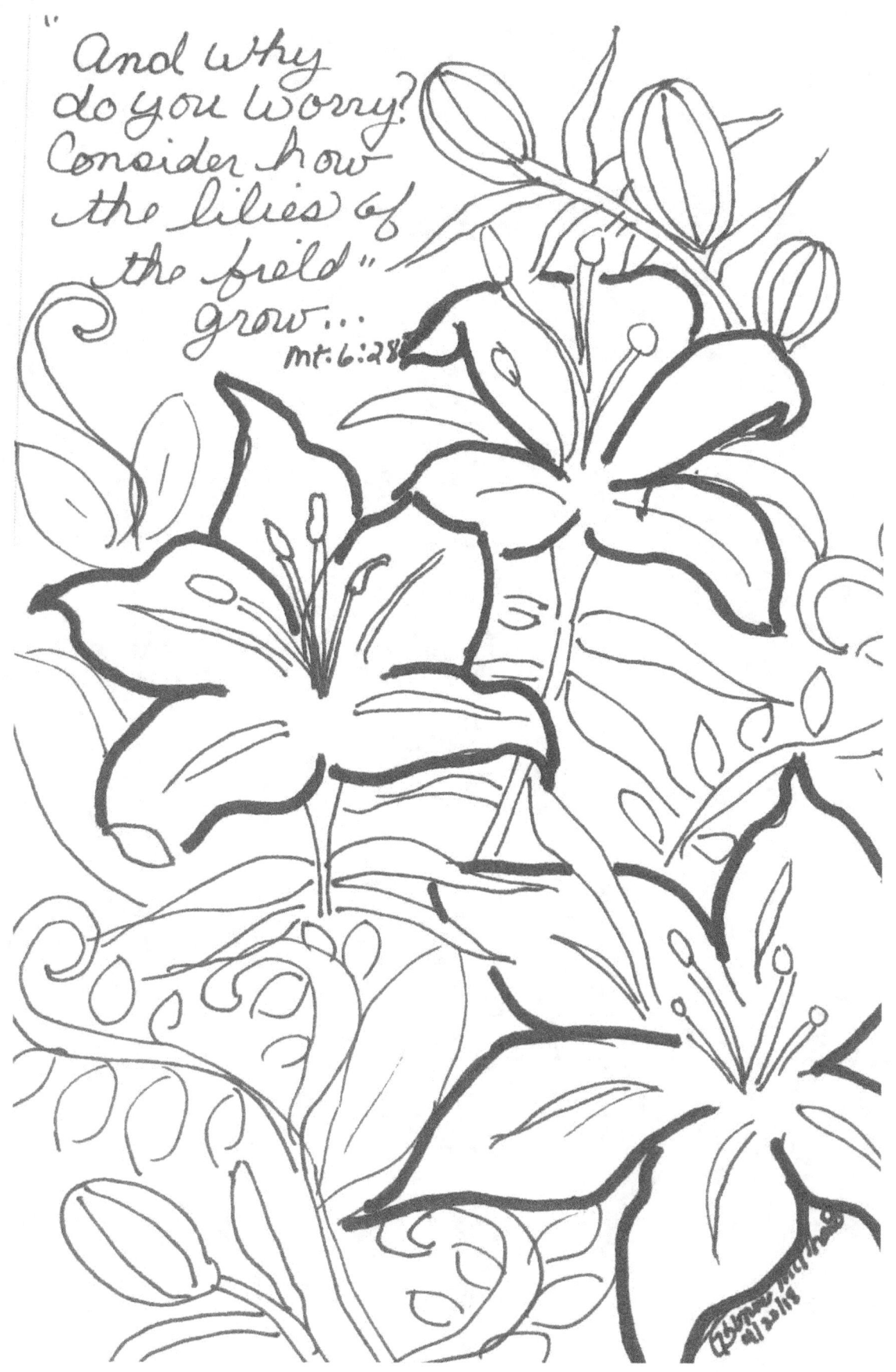

"And why do you worry? Consider how the lilies of the field" grow...
mt. 6:28

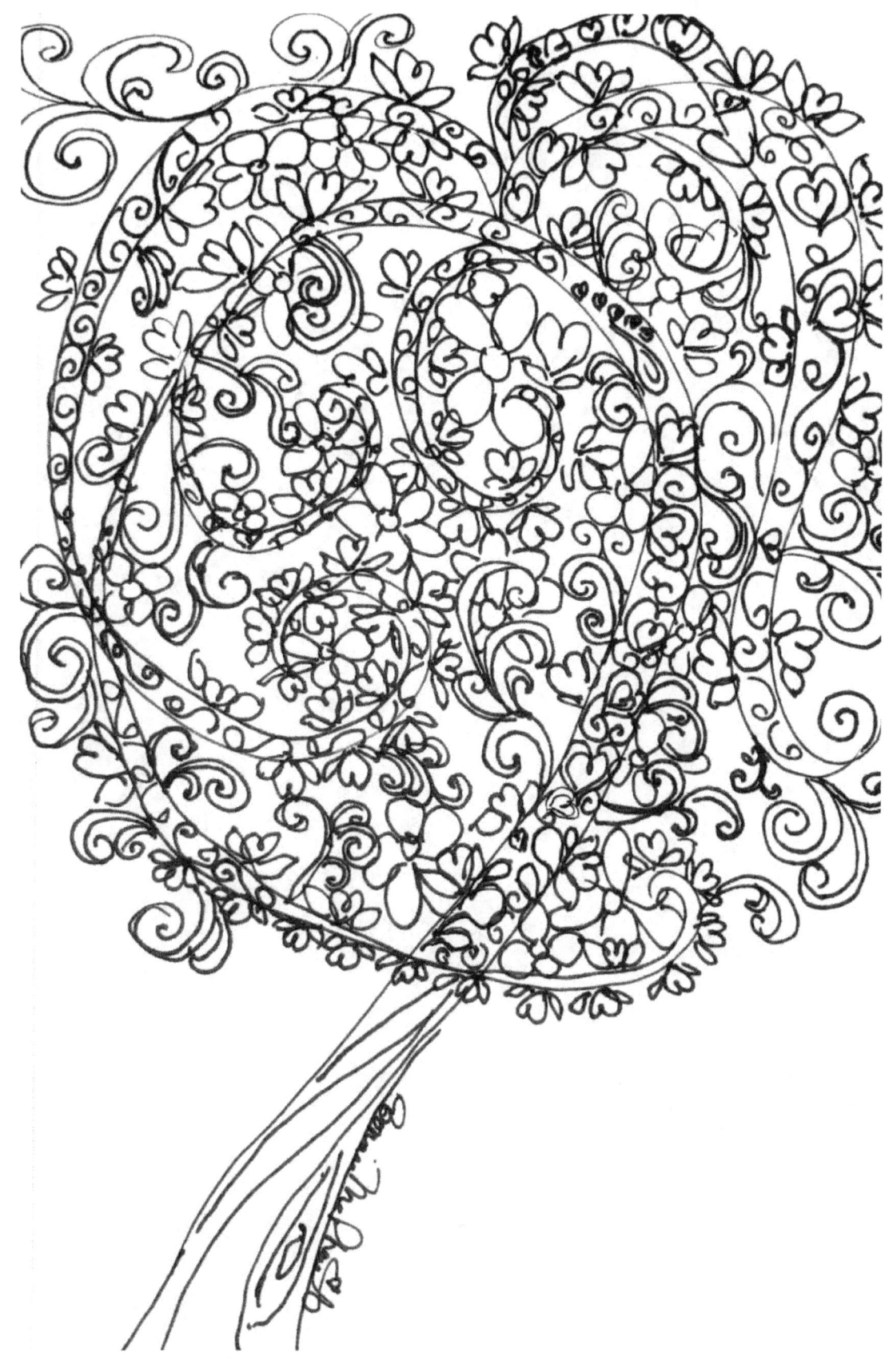

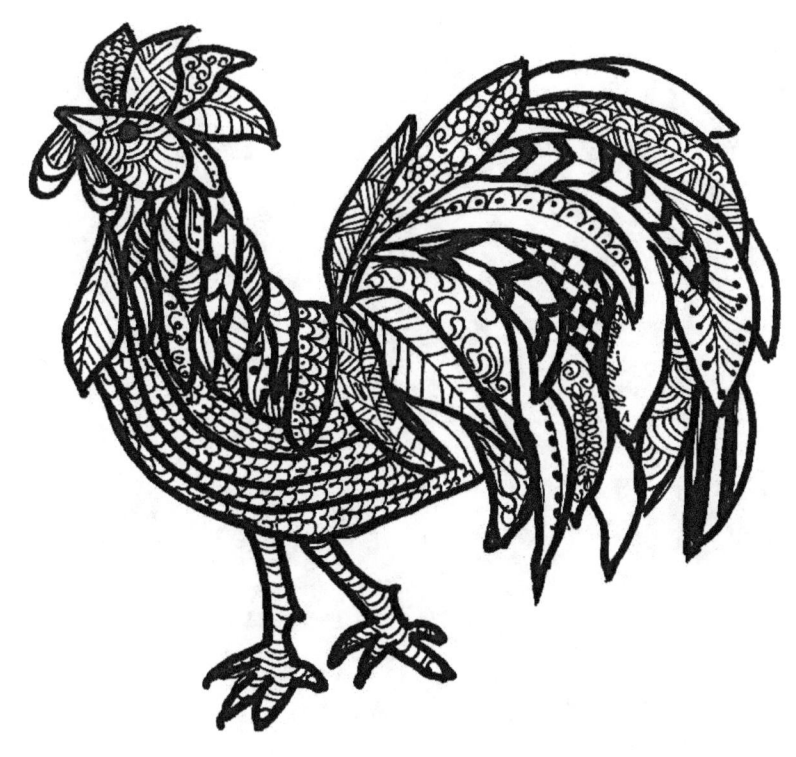

"You search out my path and my lying down and are acquainted with all
my ways. Even before a word is on my tongue, behold,
O LORD, you know it all together."
Psalm 139:3-4

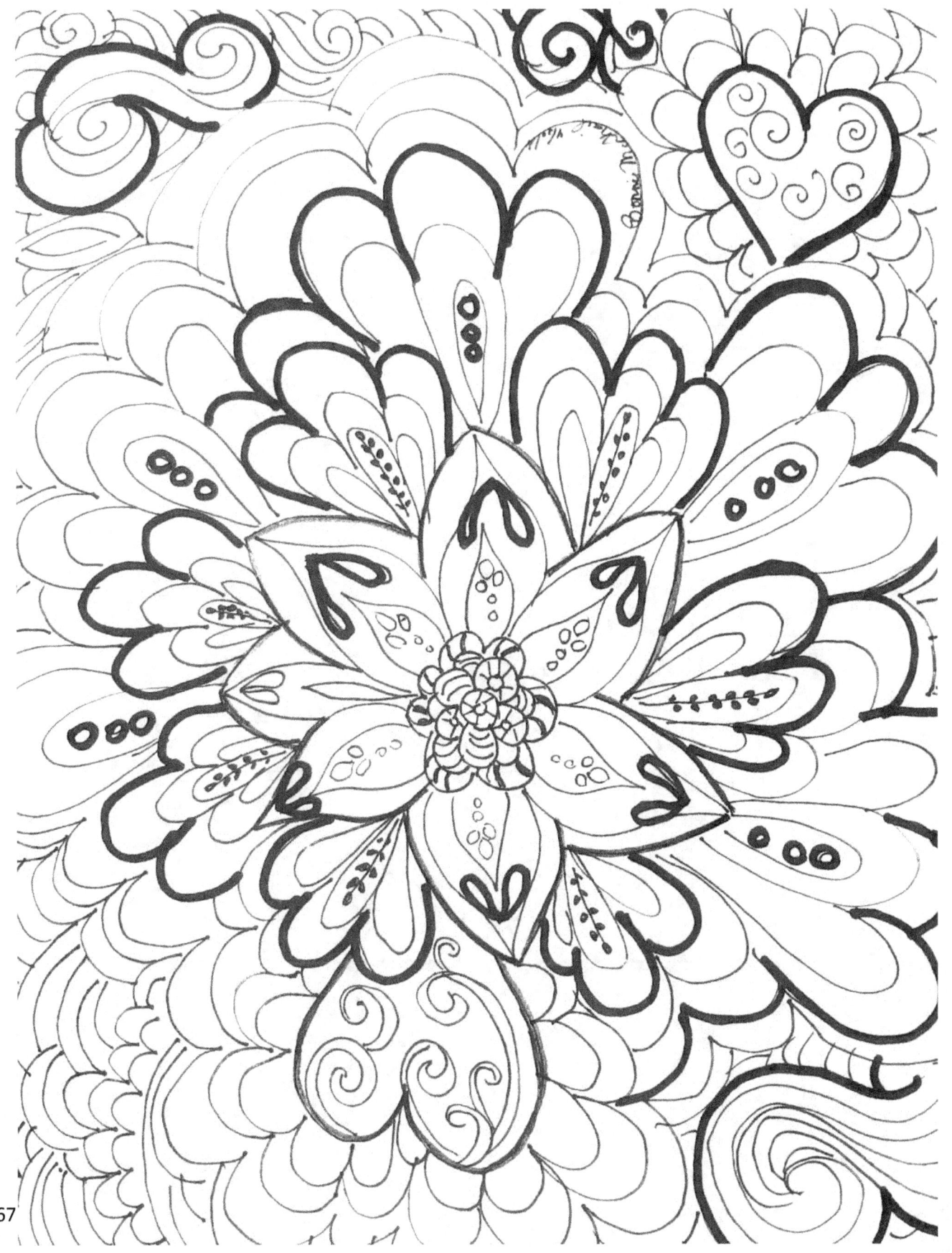

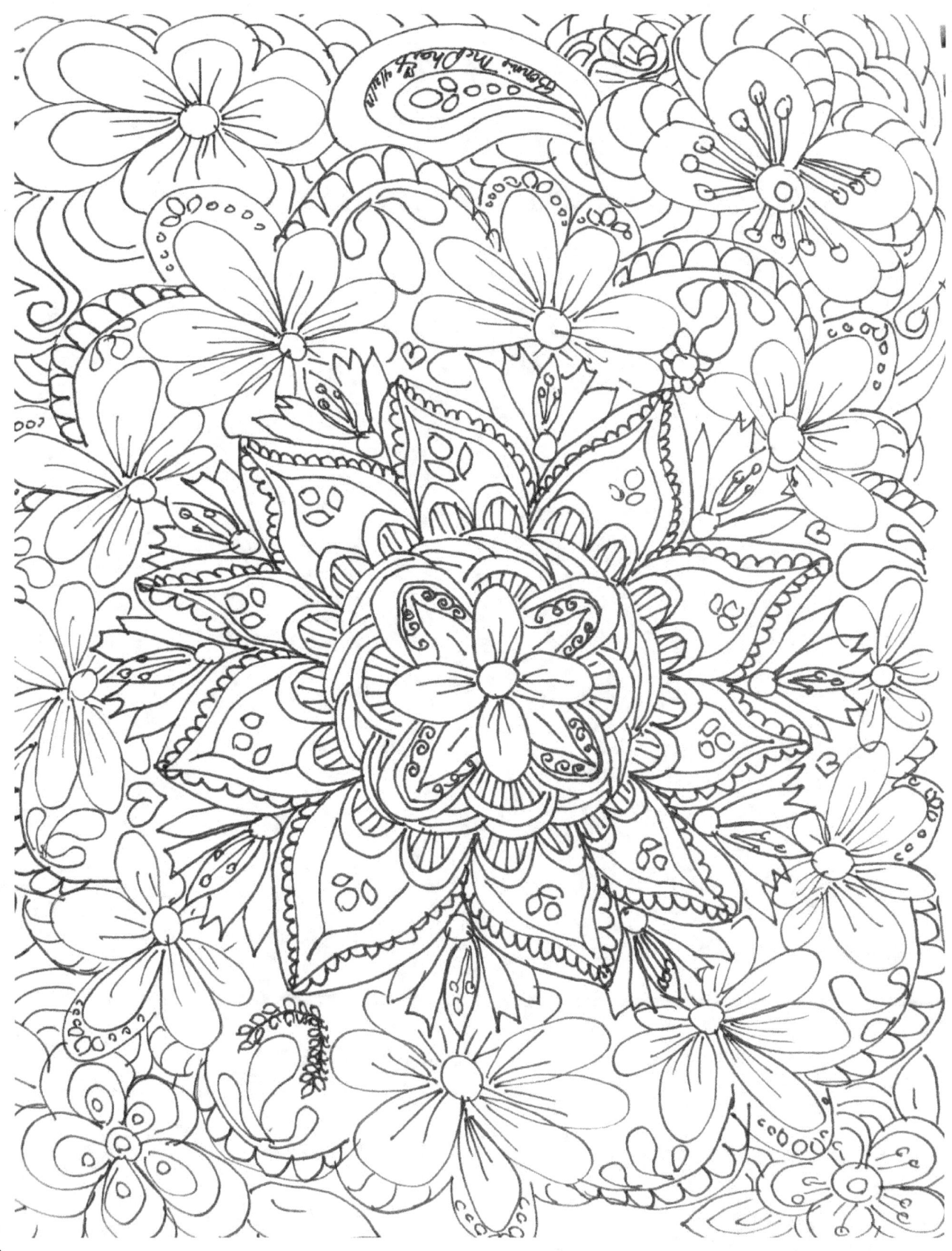

69

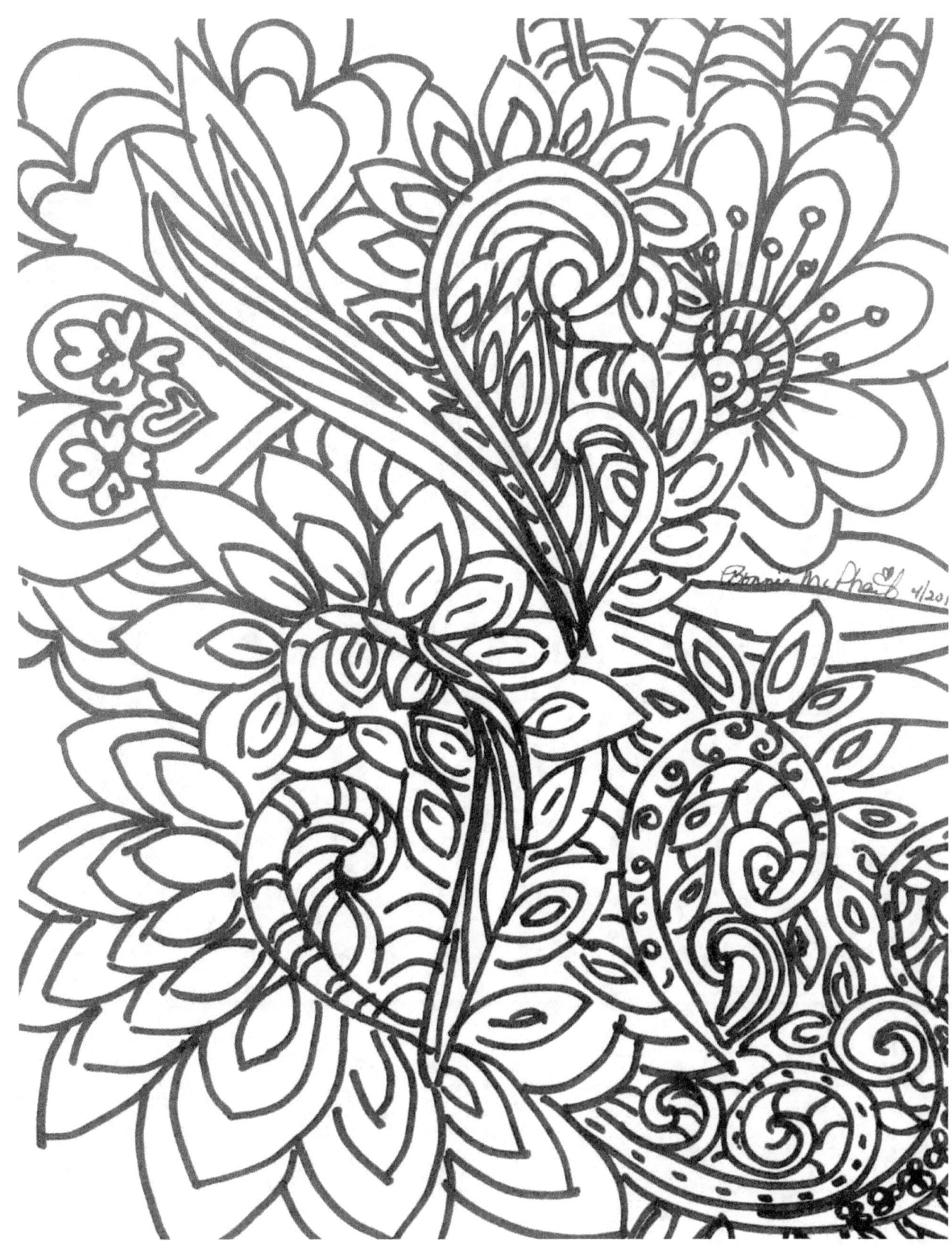

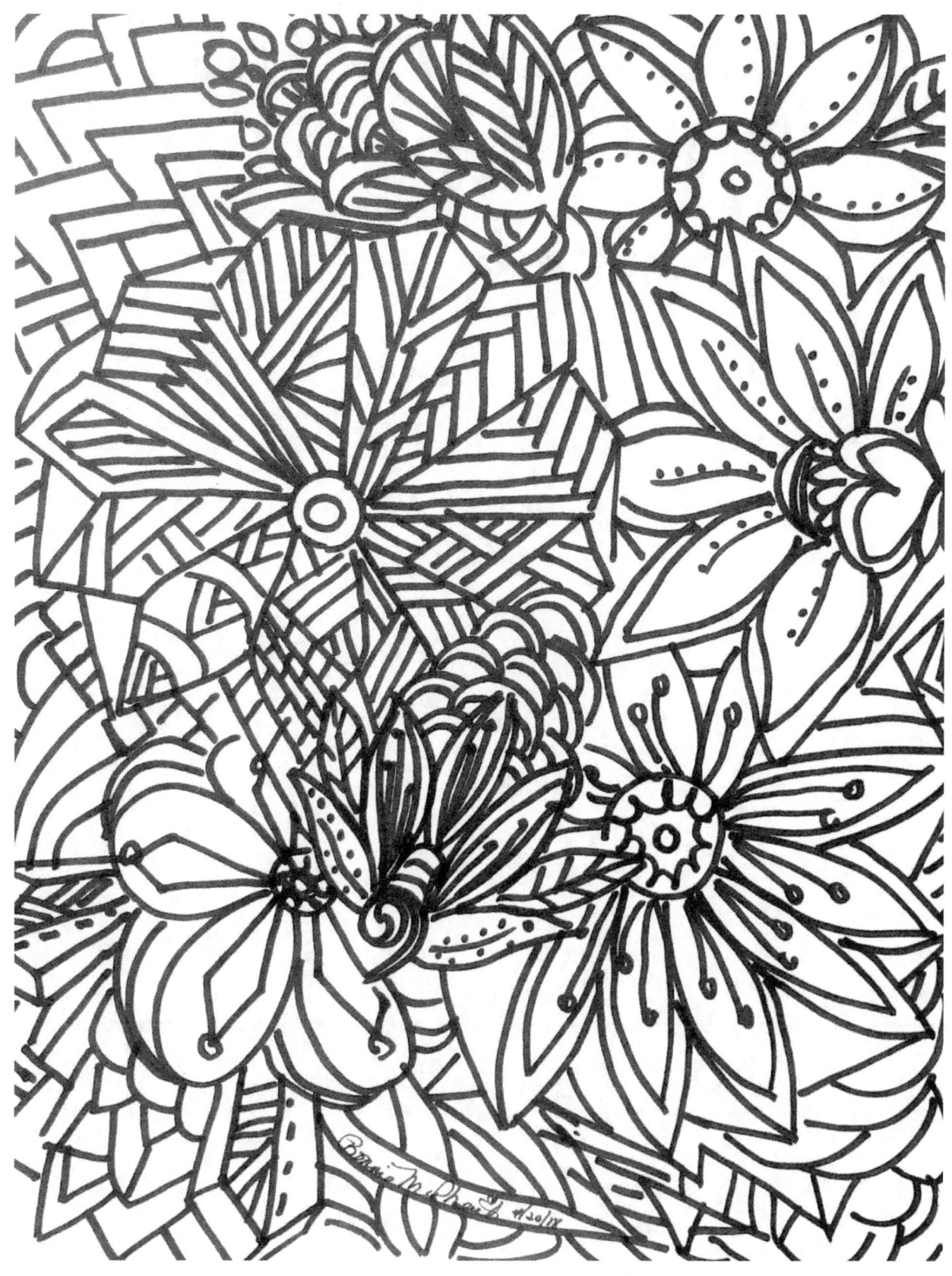

"Bless the
Lord, O my Soul,
and all
that is within
me, bless His
holy name"
psalm 103:1

"I will sing to the LORD as long as I live; I will sing praise to my God while I have my being."

Psalm 104:33

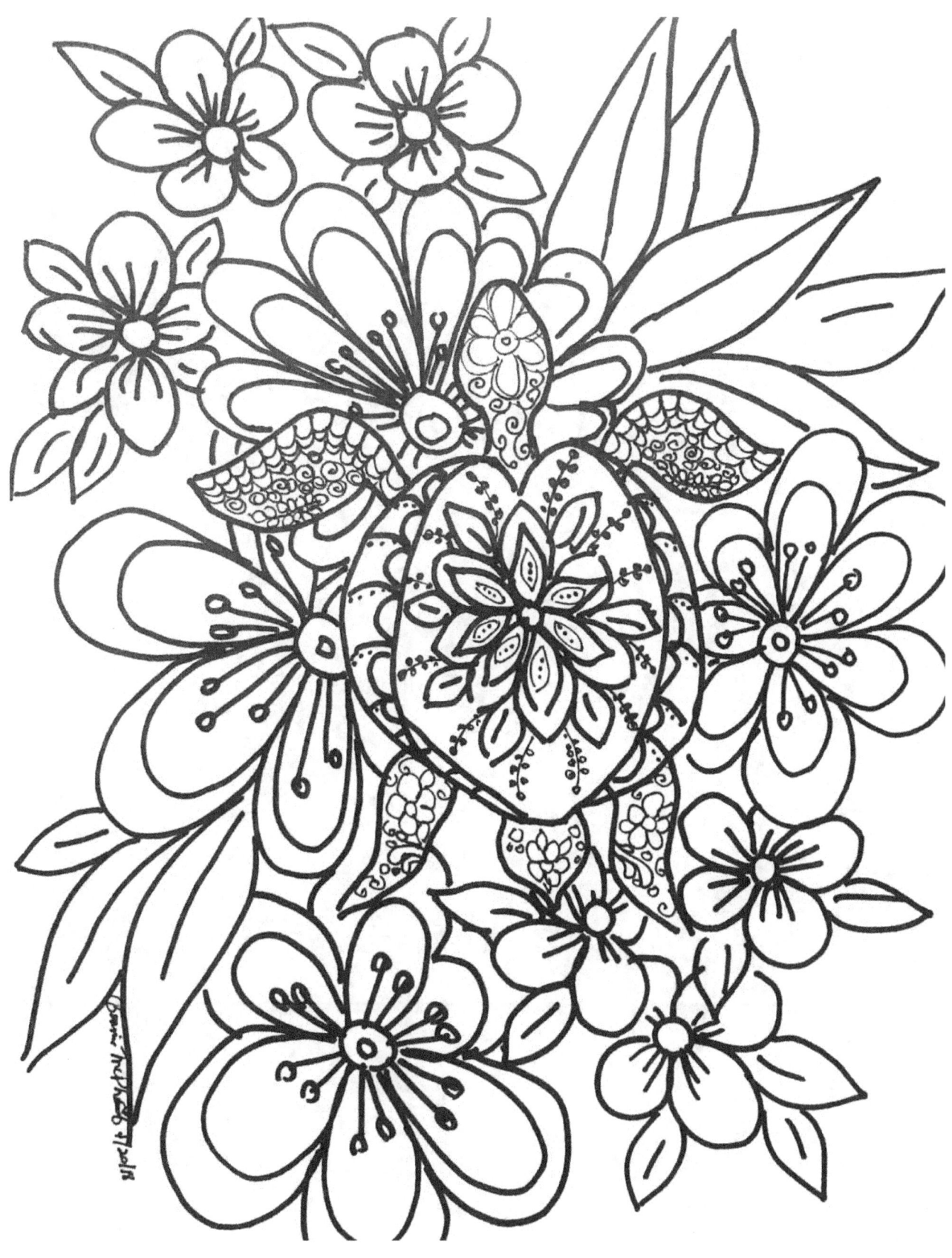

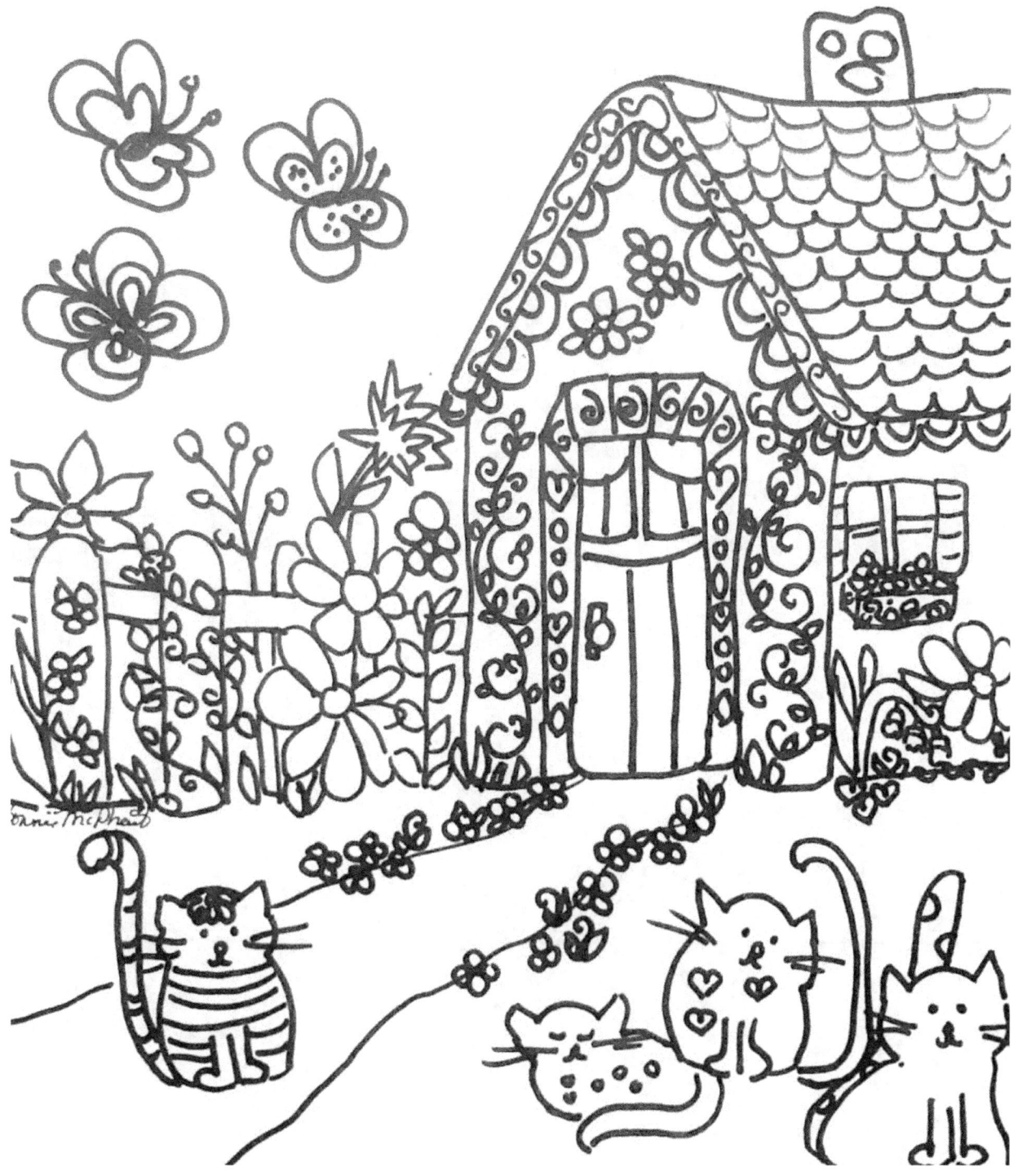

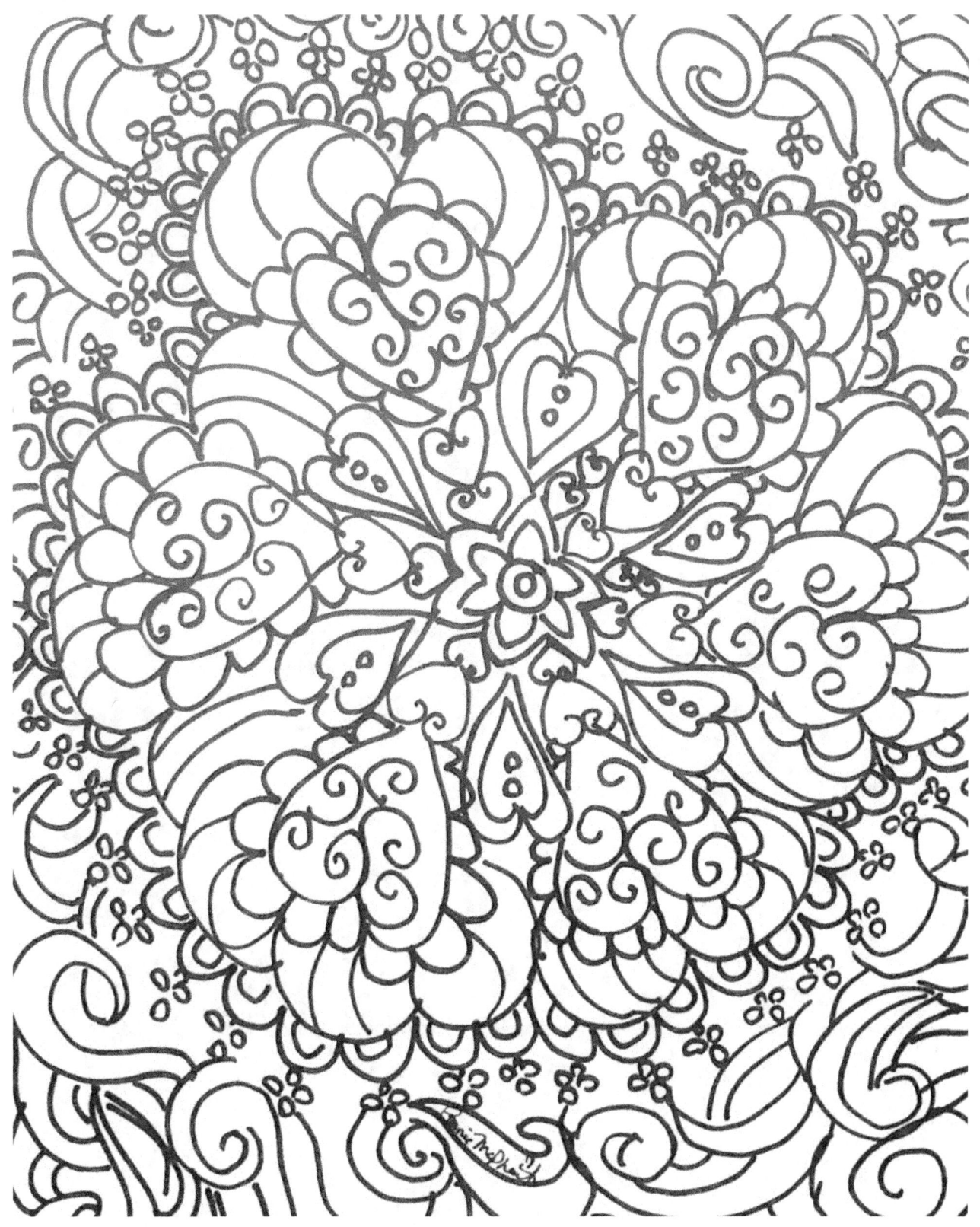

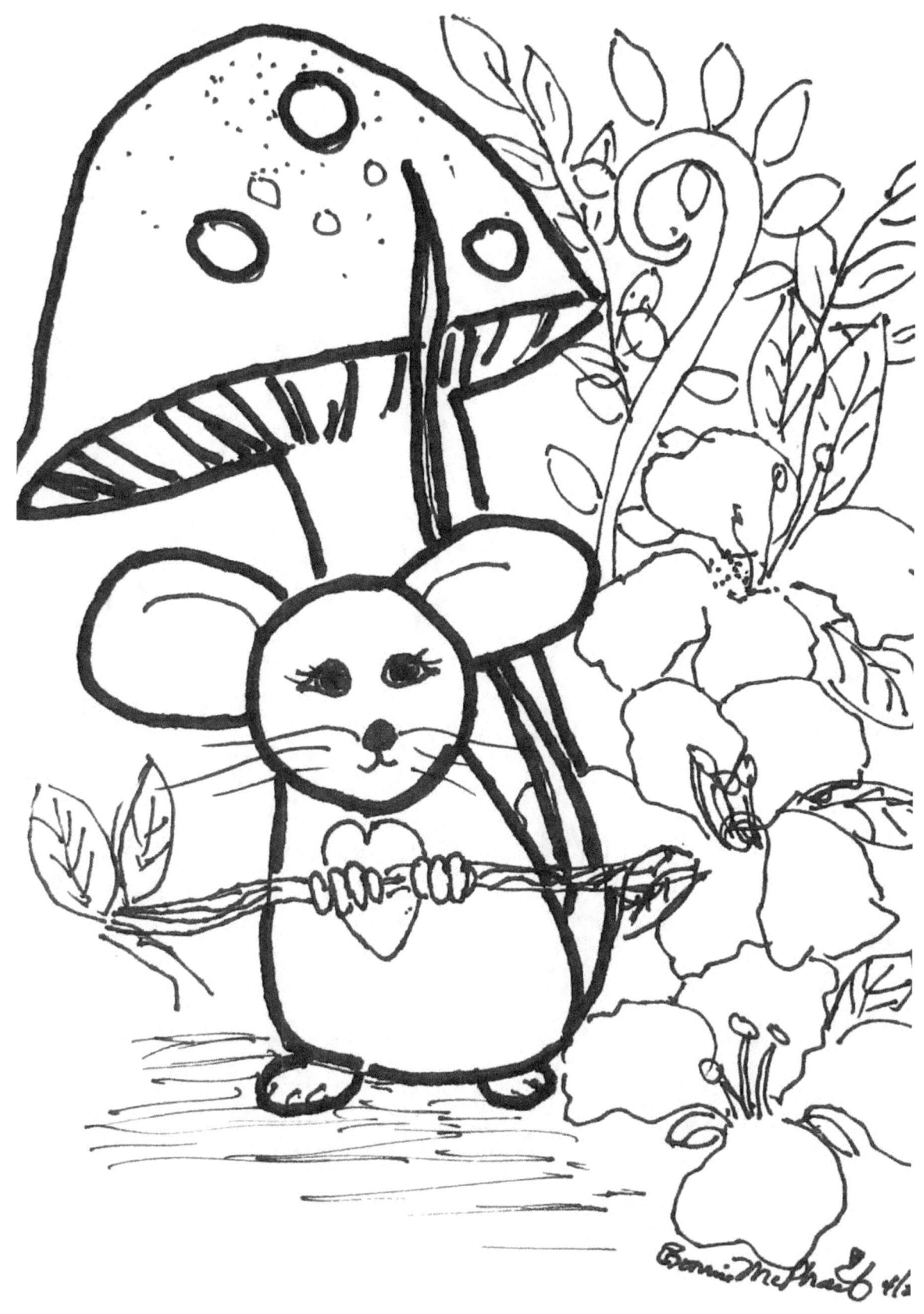

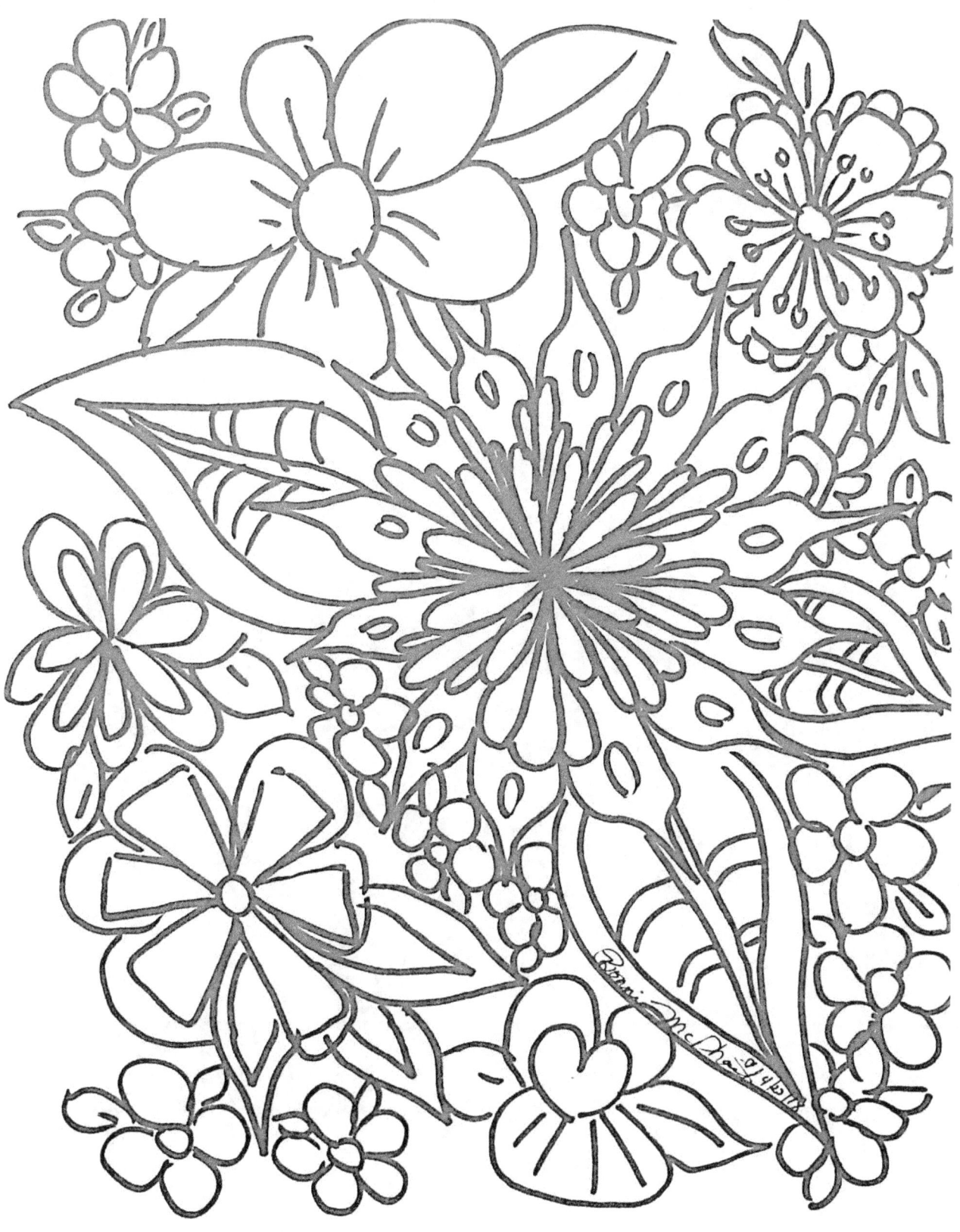

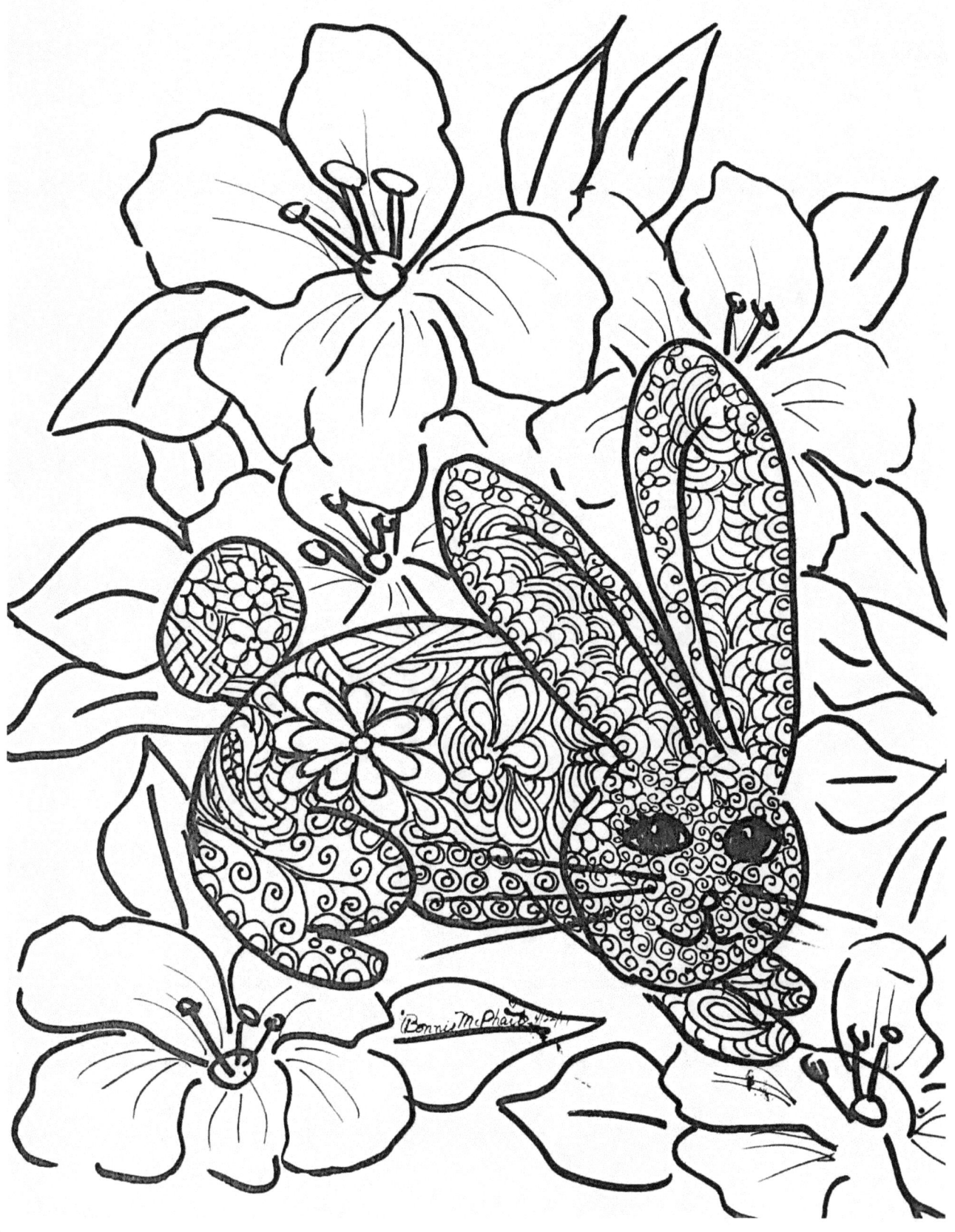

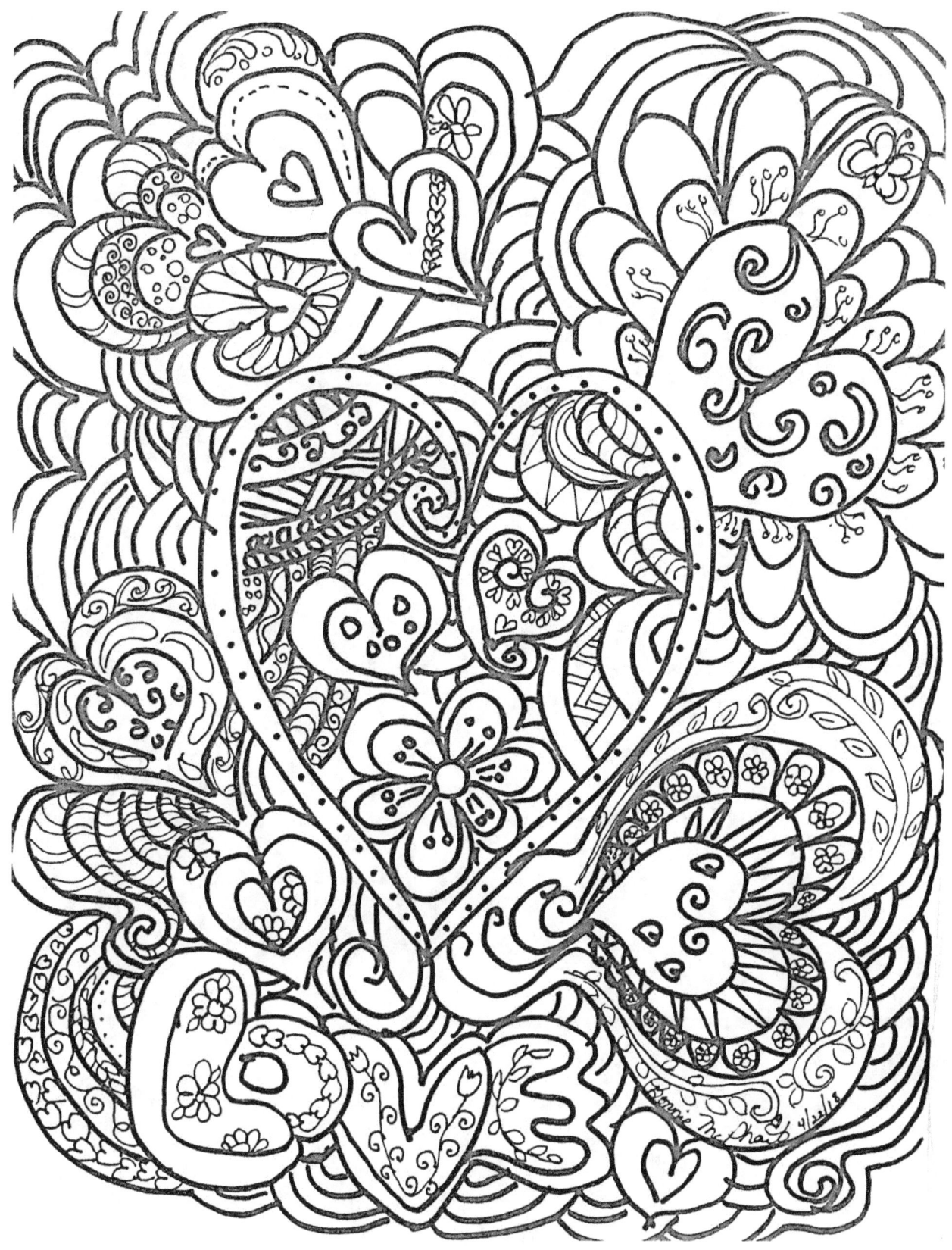

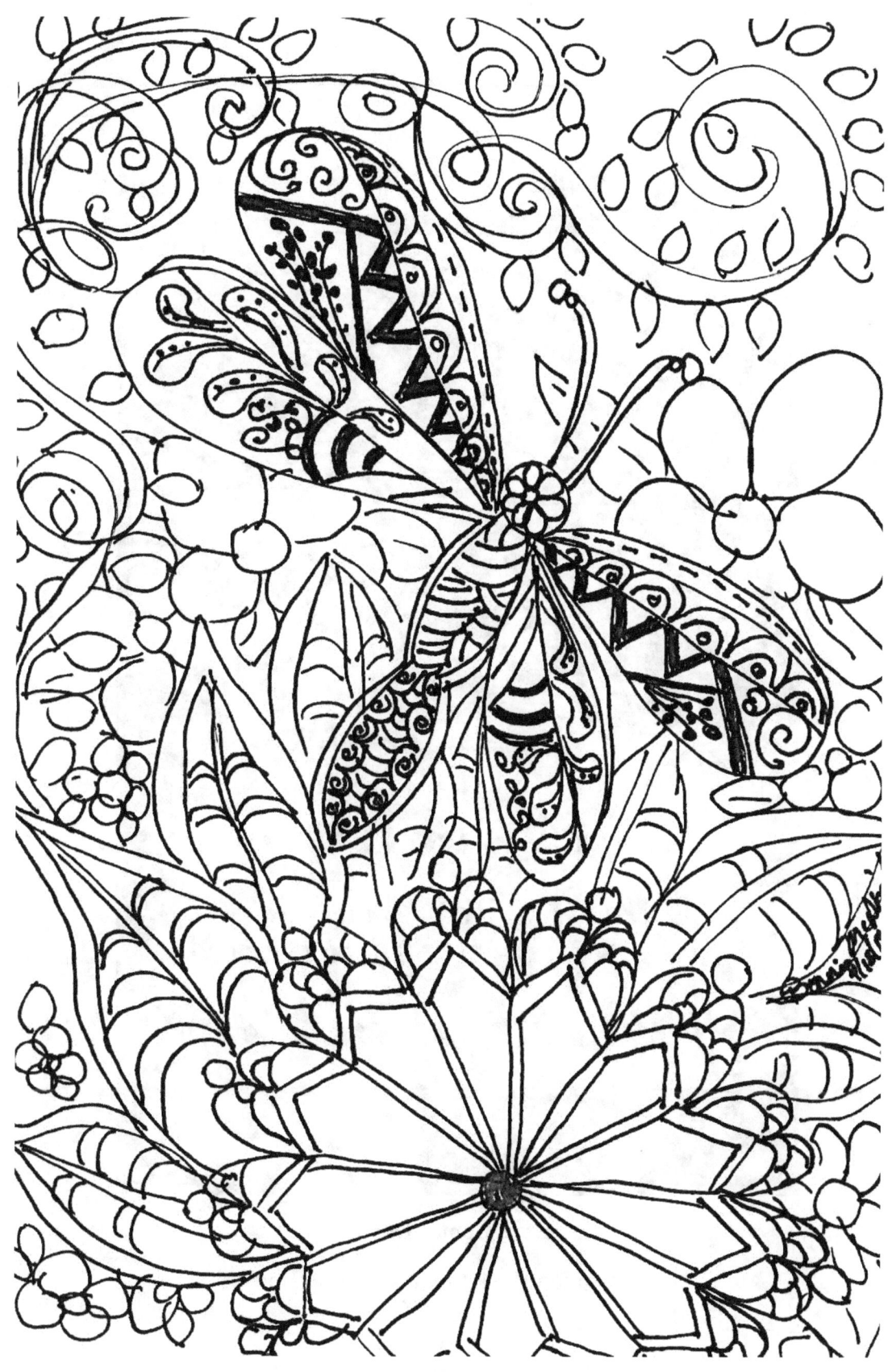

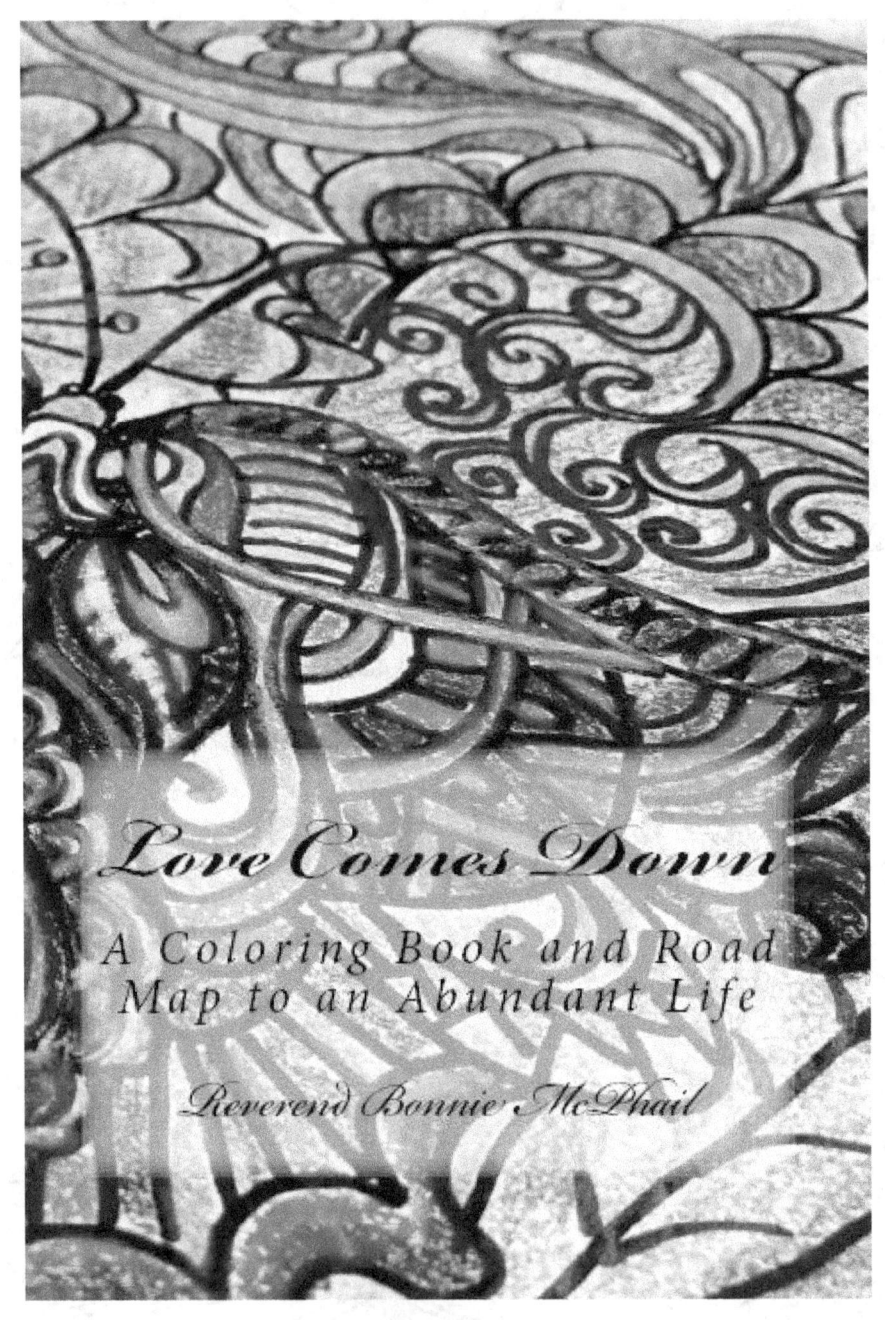

Love Comes Down

A Coloring Book and Road
Map to an Abundant Life

Reverend Bonnie McPhail

Love Comes Down

Companion Book to this Coloring Book

Dear Friends,

This is my personal favorite out of all hundred or more books the Lord has graced me to write. It is by far the best and most important work.

This book combines personal inspirational life stories and actual encounters with angels, there are places for you to write your thoughts and prayers and a daily devotional. This book also contains over 60 pages of original artwork for you to color and make your own, even the headers at the top of each page are designed to be colored in. The pieces are integrated throughout the book with many at the end of the book that have a blank space to write your thoughts, dreams, ideas and prayers. A keepsake to go back and see what the Lord was doing in your life of your own thoughts idea, dreams, prayers, and I promise you the Lord will speak personally and directly to you as you spend time in the pages of this book.

This book is designed not to just read but to truly be a rich, meaningful and powerful experience.

In the pages of this book you will work through one simple prayer a day along with a daily devotional that I was given directly from the angels just for you, and there will be personal journal entries along with activities including the coloring book pages that will lead you into a deep inner work so that you might experience the glories of all that God has for you.

I will guide you step by step along the way by using my own personal stories as a launch pad for you to experience your own.

I do not profess to have any ability in myself. The Lord has directed me to do this for your benefit. He loves you so very much! I am just an obedient vessel who is willing to take the time to listen and I write what I hear. So all the credit goes to my Lord and Savior Jesus where it belongs.

This book will bring enlightenment, encouragement, inspiration and make the scriptures come alive. I will teach you how to wage war in prayer and stand on the word of God and also how to "see" into the heavenlies. You are getting ready to encounter the Lord in a way like none other. You just have to be open and willing. God gives the most amazing and profound gifts and I cannot wait to share this with you!

I promise you God will speak directly to you. He has a specific and wonderfully unique plan for your life.

God loves you. He wants to speak to you. He wants to guide, direct and answer your prayers, he wants to take you right into the heavenlies and experiences the glories of heaven for yourself. He has an amazing plan for your life!

Love comes down and meets us right where we are. May he grant every heart's desire, bring you delight, and reveal amazing truths as you work through this book!

Blessings dear friends, from my heart to yours…

Pastor Bonnie

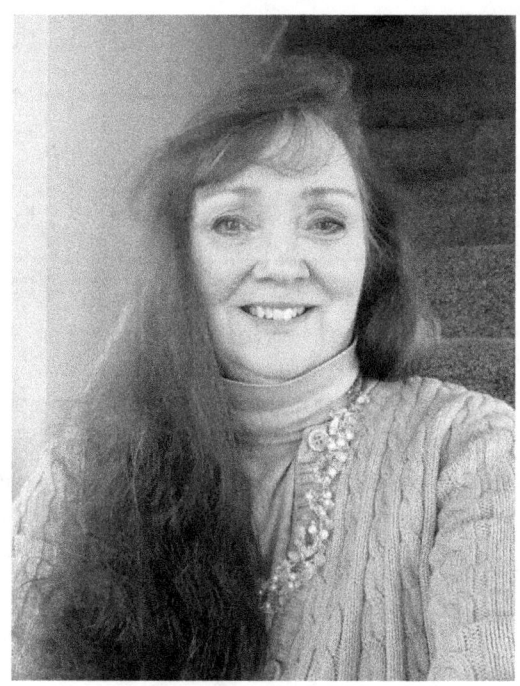

About the Author

Reverend Bonnie McPhail has a B.S. in Organizational Management and Ethics, an A.S.N. in Nursing, and certifications both in pastoral studies and life coaching. She is an ordained Assembly of God minister. Her nursing background gives her special insight into the emotional and physical needs of women, and she serves as a pastor to women when she ministers to them. Her work has been published both nationally and internationally, and she is available for conferences and workshops.

You can contact her via email if you would like to schedule a class or workshop at angelcare6@yahoo.com

"For this is how God loved the world: He gave his one and only Son, so that everyone who believes in him will not perish but have eternal life. God sent his son into the world not to judge the world, but to save the world through him." John 3:16 NLT Ask Jesus into your heart he will give you new life! He loves you!